The RSC Shakespeare

WILLIAM SHAKESPEARE

A MIDSUMMER NIGHT'S DREAM

Edited by
Jonathan Bate and Eric Rasmussen

Introduced by Jonathan Bate

Macmillan

Published by arrangement with Modern Library, an imprint of The Random House Publishing Group, a division of Random House, Inc.

Published 2008 by
MACMILLAN PUBLISHERS LTD
Houndmills, Basingstoke, Hampshire RG21 6XS
Companies and representatives throughout the world

ISBN-13   978–0–230–21788–1 hardback
ISBN-13   978–0–230–21789–8 paperback

This book is printed on paper suitable for recycling and made from fully managed and sustained forest sources.

A catalogue record for this book is available from the British Library.

10   9   8   7   6   5   4   3
17   16   15   14   13   12

Printed in China

A MIDSUMMER NIGHT'S DREAM

The RSC Shakespeare

Edited by Jonathan Bate and Eric Rasmussen

Chief Associate Editor: Héloïse Sénéchal

Associate Editors: Trey Jansen, Eleanor Lowe, Lucy Munro, Dee Anna Phares, Jan Sewell

A Midsummer Night's Dream

Textual editing: Eric Rasmussen

Introduction and Shakespeare's Career in the Theatre: Jonathan Bate

Commentary: Eleanor Lowe and Héloïse Sénéchal

Scene-by-Scene Analysis: Esme Miskimmin

In Performance: Karin Brown (RSC stagings) and Jan Sewell (overview)

The Director's Cut (interviews by Jonathan Bate and Kevin Wright): Michael Boyd, Gregory Doran and Tim Supple

CONTENTS

INTRODUCTION

Shakespeare is the poet of double vision. The father of twins, he was a mingler of comedy and tragedy, low life and high, prose and verse. He was a countryman who worked in the city, a teller of English folktales who was equally versed in the mythology of ancient Greece and Rome. His mind and world were poised between Catholicism and Protestantism, old feudal ways and new bourgeois ambitions, rational thinking and visceral instinct. *A Midsummer Night's Dream* is one of his truly essential works because nowhere else is his double vision more apparent than in this play's movement between the city and the wood, day and night, reason and imagination, waking life and dream.

MAGICAL THINKING

Wood, night, imagination, dream. These are the co-ordinates of the second form of sight, which is best described as magical thinking. It is the mode of being that belongs to visionaries, astrologers, 'wise women' and poets. It conjures up a world animated with energies and spirit forces; it finds correspondences between earthly things and divine. The eye that sees in this way rolls 'in a fine frenzy', as Theseus says, glancing 'from heaven to earth, from earth to heaven'. It 'bodies forth / The forms of things unknown', 'turns them to shapes and gives to airy nothing / A local habitation and a name.'

Magical thinking answers a deep human need. It is a way of making sense of things that would otherwise seem painfully arbitrary – things like love and beauty. An ugly birthmark on a baby would be explained away by the suggestion that the infant might be a 'changeling child', swapped in the cradle by some night-tripping fairy. The sheer chance involved in the process of what we now call sexual chemistry may be rationalized in the story of the magic properties of the juice of the flower called love-in-idleness. And in a world dependent on an agricultural economy, bad harvests were somehow more palatable if explained by the intervention of malicious sprites upon the vicissitudes of the weather.

In the age of candle and rush-light, nights were seriously dark. The night was accordingly imagined to be seriously different from the day. The very fact of long hours of light itself conferred a kind of magic upon Midsummer Night. This is the night of the year when magical thinking is given full rein. For centuries, the summer solstice had been a festive occasion celebrated with bonfires, feasting and merrymaking.

Theseus and Hippolyta never meet Oberon and Titania. In the original performance, the respective roles were likely to have been doubled. The contentious king and queen of fairies thus become the dark psychological doubles of the betrothed courtly couple. The correspondence inevitably calls into question the joy of the match between Athenian and Amazon. Oberon actually accuses Titania of having led Theseus 'through the glimmering night' when he deserted 'Perigenia whom he ravishèd', of having made the day duke break faith with a succession of paramours. Shakespeare loves to set up an antithesis, then knock it down. Here he implies that there is ultimately no sharp distinction between day and night: the sexual ethics of Theseus are perhaps as dubious as those of the adulterous child-possessor Titania.

Authority figures, representatives of the day world of political power, win little sympathy in *A Midsummer Night's Dream*. For the lovers, the forest may be a place of confused identity, but at least it is an escape from the patriarchal match-making of Egeus. In the audience, the characters with whom we engage most warmly are neither monarchs nor lords, but the mischief-making Robin Good-fellow and the ineffable weaver, Bottom. Each in his way is an embodiment of the theatrical spirit that animates everything that is most gloriously Shakespearean. Always a man of the theatre,

Shakespeare lives in a world of illusion and make-believe that hits at deepest truths; he knows that his world is fundamentally sympathetic to those other counter-worlds which we call dream and magic.

Robin the Puck compares the mortals to fools in a fond pageant: he has a right to think of himself as author of the play, since it is his dispensing of the love juice that fuels the plot. As for Bottom, at one level he is a bad actor. In both rehearsal and performance of 'Pyramus and Thisbe', it becomes clear that he does not really understand the rules of the theatrical game. But at a deeper level, he is a true dramatic genius: he is gifted with the child's grace to suspend his disbelief. As Pyramus, he puts up a pretty poor performance; as Ass, it is another matter. The comic deficiency of 'Pyramus and Thisbe' is that the actors keep telling us that they *haven't* become their characters. The Assification of Bottom is, by contrast, akin to those brilliant assumptions of disguise – Rosalind becoming Ganymede in *As You Like It*, Viola as Cesario in *Twelfth Night* – through which Shakespeare simultaneously reminds us that we are in the theatre (an actor is always in disguise) and helps us to forget where we are (we willingly suspend our disbelief). In that forgetting, we participate in the mystery of magical thinking. With Bottom himself, we in the audience may say 'I have had a most rare vision.'

Many members of Shakespeare's original audience, steeped as they were in the New Testament, would have recognized Bottom's account of his dream as an allusion – with the attributes of the different senses comically garbled – to a famous passage in the first Epistle to the Corinthians, in which St Paul says that the eye of man has not seen and the ear of man has not heard the glories that will await us when we enter the Kingdom of Heaven. In the Geneva translation of the Bible, which Shakespeare knew well, the passage speaks of how the human spirit searches 'the bottom of God's secrets'. Jesus said that in order to enter his kingdom, one had to make oneself as a child. The same may be said of the kingdom of theatre. It is because Bottom has the uncynical, believing spirit of a child that he is vouchsafed his vision. At the same time, Shakespeare himself offers a dangerously grown up image of what heaven might be like: the weaver may be innocent but the fairy queen is an embodiment of sexual experience. The 'virgin queen' Elizabeth was also known as England's 'fairy queen' and the wood in which the action takes place, with its 'nine men's morris' and English wild flowers, is more domestic than Athenian, so there must have been an inherent political risk in the representation of a sexually voracious Titania. Shakespeare perhaps introduced Oberon's apparent allusion to a chaste Elizabeth – the 'fair vestal thronèd by the west' – in order to dismiss any identification of Titania with the real-life fairy queen whom he knew would at some point be a spectator of the play.

METAMORPHOSIS

The comedy and the charm of the *Dream* depend on a certain fragility. Good comedy is tragedy narrowly averted, while fairy charm is only safe from sentimentality if attached to some potential for the grotesque. Fairies only deserve to be believed in when they have the capacity to be seriously unpleasant. Of course we laugh when Bottom wears the head of an ass and makes love to a queen, but the image deliberately courts the suggestion of bestiality.

In Ovid's *Metamorphoses*, Shakespeare's favourite book and the source for the tale of 'Pyramus and Thisbe', people are driven by bestial desires and are rewarded by being transformed into animals. In Shakespeare, the ass's head is worn in play, but it remains the closest thing in the drama of his age to an actual animal metamorphosis on stage.

Ovid was rational Rome's great counter-visionary, its magical thinker. His theme is transformation, the inevitability of change. Book fifteen of the *Metamorphoses* offers a philosophical discourse on the subject, mediated via the philosophy of Pythagoras. From here Shakespeare got many of those images of transience that roll through his Sonnets, but in the *Dream* he celebrates the transfiguring and enduring power of night vision, of second sight.

Night is the time for fantasy and for love, the time in which your wildest hopes may be indulged but your worst nightmares may have to be confronted. The action in the forest fills the space between the betrothal and the wedding celebration of Theseus and Hippolyta. For the young lovers it is also a time-between, the time, that is to say, of maturation, of discovering who they really are and whom they really love. When Hermia and Lysander, Helena and Demetrius emerge after a Midsummer Night's madness in the wood, they don't quite know what's happened: 'Methinks I see these things with parted eye, / When everything seems double.' And they're not all quite sure if they've finally gained the person they want: 'And I have found Demetrius like a jewel, / Mine own and not mine own.' But on reflection in the cold light of morning, the strangeness of the night has effected a material transformation, leading the lovers to a truer place than the one where they were at court the day before. Perhaps because she is herself a 'stranger', an outsider in the 'civilized' world of Athens, it is the Amazon queen Hippolyta who understands this best:

> But all the story of the night told over,
> And all their minds transfigured so together,
> More witnesseth than fancy's images,
> And grows to something of great constancy;
> But howsoever, strange and admirable.

THE FESTIVE WORLD

Shortly after the Second World War, the Canadian literary critic Northrop Frye published a short essay that inaugurated the modern understanding that Shakespeare's comedies, for all their lightness and play, are serious works of art, every bit as worthy of close attention as his tragedies. Entitled 'The Argument of Comedy', it proposed that the essential structure of Shakespearean comedy was ultimately derived from the 'new comedy' of ancient Greece, which was mediated to the Renaissance via its Roman exponents Plautus and Terence. The 'new comedy' pattern, described by Frye as 'a comic Oedipus situation', turned on 'the successful effort of a young man to outwit an opponent and possess the girl of his choice'.* The girl's father, or some other authority figure of the older generation, resists the match, but is outflanked, often thanks to an ingenious scheme devised by a clever servant, perhaps involving disguise or flight (or both). Frye, writing during Hollywood's golden age, saw an unbroken line from the classics to Shakespeare to modern romantic comedy: 'The average movie of today is a rigidly conventionalized New Comedy proceeding toward an act which, like death in Greek tragedy, takes place offstage, and is symbolized by the final embrace.'

The union of the lovers brings 'a renewed sense of social integration', expressed by some kind of festival at the climax of the play – a marriage, a dance or a feast. All right-thinking people come over to the side of the lovers, but there are others 'who are in some kind of mental bondage, who are helplessly driven by ruling passions, neurotic compulsions, social rituals, and selfishness'. Malvolio in *Twelfth Night*, Don John in *Much Ado about Nothing*, Jaques in *As You Like It*, Shylock in *The Merchant of Venice*: Shakespearean comedy frequently includes a party-pooper, a figure who refuses to be assimilated into the harmony. *A Midsummer Night's Dream* is his most joyous ending because there is no such figure here. At the outset, the fairies have been associated with chaos and disruption (mischief, rough weather, marital discord), but at the end they bring 'blessing' and the restoring of 'amends'.

Even here, though, one might wonder in retrospect whether all has quite ended well. The closing song expresses the hope that the children of all three united couples will not suffer 'the blots of Nature's hand', that they will not be marked by 'hare-lip, nor scar' nor any other ill-boding deformation. The very act of warding off such portents brings their possibility into play, and the mythologi-cally literate audience member might recall that the child of Theseus and Hippolyta would be Hippolytus. Some disturbing associations then become apparent: the Theseus of ancient Greek myth would desert Hippolyta and marry Phaedra, sister of Ariadne (whom, as the

---

* 'The Argument of Comedy', first published in *English Institute Essays 1948*, ed. D. A. Robertson (1949). This article has often been reprinted in critical anthologies, and Frye himself adapted it for inclusion in his classic study, *Anatomy of Criticism* (1957).

play reminds us, he had earlier seduced and deserted, after she had assisted him with the thread that led him out of the labyrinth after he had slain the Minotaur). Phaedra would fall in love with her stepson Hippolytus, a young man more interested in hunting than women. She would falsely accuse him of raping her and then commit suicide. Blaming his son, Theseus would exile Hippolytus, who would promptly be thrown to his death when his horse ran wild with fear as a bull-like monster rose from the sea. That monster is a reminder of the Minotaur, the monster in the labyrinth with the head of a bull and the body of a man, who was the fruit of the perverted sexual union between a white bull sent by the sea-god and Queen Pasiphaë, the mother of Ariadne and Phaedra.

Neither Hippolytus nor Phaedra is mentioned in the play. Yet the wish in the final fairy song for the issue of Theseus and Hippolyta to be 'fortunate', coupled with the play's earlier enactment of the love-making between a queen and a beast (not to mention the reference to Theseus' history as a serial seducer and deserter of women), means that the tragic history surrounding the mythological prototypes of the characters is not entirely absent. Seneca's *Hippolytus* was one of the best-known classical tragedies in the sixteenth century and its hunting imagery seems to inform the play. As so often with Shakespeare, the context may be understood in diametrically opposed ways. Perhaps he is taking dark subject-matter – violence, illicit desire, monstrous births – and transforming it into something life-affirming, emptying it of all sinister content, just as the play performed by Peter Quince and friends takes another tragic tale from classical mythology, that of Pyramus and Thisbe, and fills it with 'mirth'. Or perhaps he is suggesting that, however joyous comedy's climactic festivity may be, it offers only a momentary suspension of life's complications. Midsummer Night, May Day, Twelfth Night, the feast of fools in which for an evening the master becomes the servant and vice versa: these festive occasions are celebrations of life and social harmony, but they end in the knowledge that tomorrow we will have to go back to work, to the hierarchies and compromises of everyday normality. 'How shall we find the concord of this discord?' asks Theseus of the paradox whereby the play of Pyramus and Thisbe is both 'merry and tragical'. Every production and every reading of *A Midsummer Night's Dream* has to make a choice as to the extent to which the 'discord' is still apparent behind the 'concord' woven by the resolution of the plot.

Northrop Frye's 'The Argument of Comedy' pinpoints a pervasive structure: 'the action of the comedy begins in a world represented as a normal world, moves into the green world, goes into a metamorphosis there in which the comic resolution is achieved, and returns to the normal world'. But for Shakespeare, the green world, the forest and its fairies, is no less real than the court. Frye, again, sums it up brilliantly:

> This world of fairies, dreams, disembodied souls, and pastoral lovers may not be a 'real' world, but, if not, there is something equally illusory in the stumbling and blinded follies of the 'normal' world, of Theseus' Athens with its idiotic marriage law, of Duke Frederick and his melancholy tyranny [in *As You Like It*], of Leontes and his mad jealousy [in *The Winter's Tale*], of the Court Party with their plots and intrigues. The famous speech of Prospero about the dream nature of reality applies equally to Milan and the enchanted island. We spend our lives partly in a waking world we call normal and partly in a dream world which we create out of our own desires. Shakespeare endows both worlds with equal imaginative power, brings them opposite one another, and makes each world seem unreal when seen by the light of the other.

'THE POET'S EYE . . . THE POET'S PEN'

At the beginning of the final act, Theseus suggests that the dream world, which we may also call the green world, is illusory, 'more strange than true', a trick of the 'strong imagination':

> More strange than true. I never may believe
> These antic fables, nor these fairy toys.
> Lovers and madmen have such seething brains,

Such shaping fantasies that apprehend
More than cool reason ever comprehends.
The lunatic, the lover and the poet
Are of imagination all compact.
One sees more devils than vast hell can hold;
That is the madman. The lover, all as frantic,
Sees Helen's beauty in a brow of Egypt.
The poet's eye, in a fine frenzy rolling,
Doth glance from heaven to earth, from earth to heaven,
And as imagination bodies forth
The forms of things unknown, the poet's pen
Turns them to shapes and gives to airy nothing
A local habitation and a name.
Such tricks hath strong imagination,
That if it would but apprehend some joy,
It comprehends some bringer of that joy.
Or in the night, imagining some fear,
How easy is a bush supposed a bear!

Multiple ironies are at work here. Theseus himself is an 'antic fable' – the adjective plays on 'bizarre/grotesque' and 'antique' (antiquated, belonging to a superannuated world of romance and mythology). And the play has suggested that fairies are not merely the invention of lunatics and lovers. Shakespeare's own loyalty must belong to 'the poet's eye' and 'the poet's pen' that keep company with the lunatic and the lover, the seething brain and the shaping fantasy. The language of poetry, like the art of the actor, is metamorphic: a play on words, a metaphor, an alliterative pairing sends the imagination leaping from a bush to a bear.

Theseus regards poetry as mere artifice, and the language of *A Midsummer Night's Dream* does indeed include many an artificial rhetorical elaboration, many a passage of highly-wrought rhyme. Yet the very speech in which Theseus expresses his scepticism about poetry embodies not only the artifice it condemns (the balancing of 'from heaven to earth, from earth to heaven', the slippage from 'apprehend' to 'comprehends'), but also a fluidity of movement – the run of the sentence structure across the line endings imposed by the metrical structure – that enacts the processes of mature thought, of what Theseus calls 'cool reason'. *A Midsummer Night's Dream* is a comedy of simultaneous innocence and experience. Of all the plays, it is the one that offers most to a child's way of seeing, and which should be everybody's introduction to Shakespeare, preferably well before the age of eleven. At the same time, it unleashes us into a world of desire that comes to the core of our adult humanity. And it is conceivably Shakespeare's most sophisticated meditation upon the power of theatre and of poetry. It is an anatomy of the very imagination by which it is created. There's magic in the web.

Selections from critical commentaries on the play, with linking narrative, are available on the edition website, www.rscshakespeare.co.uk.

ABOUT THE TEXT

Shakespeare endures through history. He illuminates later times as well as his own. He helps us to understand the human condition. But he cannot do this without a good text of the plays. Without editions there would be no Shakespeare. That is why every twenty years or so throughout the last three centuries there has been a major new edition of his complete works. One aspect of editing is the process of keeping the texts up to date – modernizing the spelling, punctuation and typography (though not, of course, the actual words), providing explanatory notes in the light of changing educational practices (a generation ago, most of Shakespeare's classical and biblical allusions could be assumed to be generally understood, but now they can't).

But because Shakespeare did not personally oversee the publication of his plays, editors also have to make decisions about the relative authority of the early printed editions. Half of the sum of his plays only appeared posthumously, in the elaborately produced First Folio text of 1623, the original 'Complete Works' prepared for the press by Shakespeare's fellow-actors, the people who knew the plays better than anyone else. The other half had appeared in print in his lifetime, in the more compact and cheaper form of 'Quarto' editions, some of which reproduced good quality texts, others of which were to a greater or lesser degree garbled and error-strewn.

Generations of editors have adopted a 'pick and mix' approach, moving between Quarto and Folio readings, making choices on either aesthetic or bibliographic grounds, sometimes creating a composite text that Shakespeare never actually wrote. Not until the 1980s did editors follow the logic of what ought to have been obvious to anyone who works in the theatre: that the Quarto and Folio texts often represent discrete moments in the life of a script, that plays change in the course of rehearsal, production and revival, and that many of the major variants between the early printed versions almost certainly reflect this process.

If you look at printers' handbooks from the age of Shakespeare, you quickly discover that one of the first rules was that, whenever possible, compositors were recommended to set their type from existing printed books rather than manuscripts. This was the age before mechanical typesetting, where each individual letter had to be picked out by hand from the compositor's case and placed on a stick (upside down and back to front) before being laid on the press. It was an age of murky rush-light and of manuscripts written in a secretary hand which had dozens of different, hard-to-decipher forms. Printers' lives were a lot easier when they were reprinting existing books rather than struggling with handwritten copy. Easily the quickest way to have created the First Folio would have been simply to reprint those eighteen plays that had already appeared in Quarto and only work from manuscript on the other eighteen.

But that is not what happened. Whenever Quartos were used, as in the case of *A Midsummer Night's Dream*, playhouse 'promptbooks' were also consulted and stage directions copied in from them. And in the case of several major plays where a well-printed Quarto was available, the Folio printers were instructed to work from an alternative, playhouse-derived manuscript. This meant that the whole process of producing the first complete Shakespeare took months, even years, longer than it might have done. But for the men overseeing the project, John Hemings and Henry Condell, friends and fellow-actors who had been remembered in Shakespeare's will, the additional labour and cost were worth the effort for the sake of producing an edition that was close to the practice of the theatre. They wanted all the plays in print so that people could, as they wrote in their prefatory address to the reader, 'read him and again and again', but they also wanted 'the great variety of readers' to work from texts that were close to the theatre-life for which Shakespeare originally intended them. For this reason, the *RSC Shakespeare*, in both *Complete Works* and individual volumes, uses the Folio as base text wherever possible. Significant Quarto variants are, however, noted in the Textual Notes.

For some specific examples of the theatre-derived changes in Folio *Midsummer Night's Dream*, see the discussion of 'Text' in 'Key Facts', below.

The following notes highlight various aspects of the editorial process and indicate conventions used in the text of this edition:

Lists of Parts are supplied in the First Folio for only six plays, not including *A Midsummer Night's Dream*, so the list here is editorially supplied. Capitals indicate that part of the name which is used for speech headings in the script (thus 'Nick BOTTOM').

Locations are provided by the Folio for only two plays, of which *A Midsummer Night's Dream* is not one. Eighteenth-century editors, working in an age of elaborately realistic stage sets, were the first to provide detailed locations ('another part of the forest'). Given that Shakespeare wrote for a bare stage and often an imprecise sense of place, we have relegated locations to the explanatory notes at the foot of the page, where they are given at the beginning of each scene where the imaginary location is different from the one before. We have emphasized broad geographical settings rather than specifics of the kind that suggest anachronistically realistic staging.

Act and Scene Divisions were provided in the Folio in a much more thoroughgoing way than in the Quartos. Sometimes, however, they were erroneous or omitted; corrections and additions supplied by editorial tradition are indicated by square brackets. Five-act division is based on a classical model, and act breaks provided the opportunity to replace the candles in the indoor Blackfriars playhouse which the King's Men used after 1608, but Shakespeare did not necessarily think in terms of a five-part structure of dramatic composition. The Folio convention is that a scene ends when the stage is empty. Nowadays, partly under the influence of film, we tend to consider a scene to be a dramatic unit that ends with either a change of imaginary location or a significant passage of time within the narrative. Shakespeare's fluidity of composition accords well with this convention, so in addition to act and scene numbers we provide a *running scene* count in the right margin at the beginning of each new scene, in the typeface used for editorial directions. Where there is a scene break caused by a momentary bare stage, but the location does not change and extra time does not pass, we use the convention *running scene continues*. There is inevitably a degree of editorial judgement in making such calls, but the system is very valuable in suggesting the pace of the plays.

Speakers' Names are often inconsistent in Folio. We have regularized speech headings, but retained an element of deliberate inconsistency in entry directions, in order to give the flavour of Folio. Thus Robin Goodfellow is always so-called in his speech headings, but is sometimes Puck in entry directions ('Puck' should probably be understood as a descriptive name, not a personal one – he is 'the puck', analogous to 'a goblin').

Verse is indicated by lines that do not run to the right margin and by capitalization of each line. The Folio printers sometimes set verse as prose, and vice versa (either out of misunderstanding or for reasons of space). We have silently corrected in such cases, although in some instances there is ambiguity, in which case we have leaned towards the preservation of Folio layout. Folio sometimes uses contraction ('turnd' rather than 'turned') to indicate whether or not the final '-ed' of a past participle is sounded, an area where there is variation for the sake of the five-beat iambic pentameter rhythm. We use the convention of a grave accent to indicate sounding (thus 'turnèd' would be two syllables), but would urge actors not to overstress. In cases where one speaker ends with a verse half-line and the next begins with the other half of the pentameter, editors since the late eighteenth century have indented the second line. We have abandoned this convention, since the Folio does not use it, and nor did actors' cues in the Shakespearean theatre. An exception is made when the second speaker actively interrupts or completes the first speaker's sentence.

Spelling is modernized, but older forms are very occasionally maintained where necessary for rhythm or aural effect.

Punctuation in Shakespeare's time was as much rhetorical as grammatical. 'Colon' was originally a term for a unit of thought in an argument. The semi-colon was a new unit of punctuation (some of the Quartos lack them altogether). We have modernized punctuation throughout, but have given more weight to Folio punctuation than many editors, since, though not Shakespearean, it reflects the usage of his period. In particular, we have used the colon far more than many editors: it is exceptionally useful as a way of indicating how many Shakespearean speeches unfold clause by clause in a developing argument that gives the illusion of enacting the process of thinking in the moment. We have also kept in mind the origin of punctuation in classical times as a way of assisting the actor and orator: the comma suggests the briefest of pauses for breath, the colon a middling one and a full stop or period a longer pause. Semi-colons, by contrast, belong to an era of punctuation that was only just coming in during Shakespeare's time and that is coming to an end now: we have accordingly only used them where they occur in our copy-texts (and not always then). Dashes are sometimes used for parenthetical interjections where the Folio has brackets. They are also used for interruptions and changes in train of thought. Where a change of addressee occurs within a speech, we have used a dash preceded by a full stop (or occasionally another form of punctuation). Often the identity of the respective addressees is obvious from the context. When it is not, this has been indicated in a marginal stage direction.

Entrances and Exits are fairly thorough in Folio, which has accordingly been followed as faithfully as possible. Where characters are omitted or corrections are necessary, this is indicated by square brackets (e.g. '[*and Attendants*]'). *Exit* is sometimes silently normalized to *Exeunt* and *Manet* anglicized to 'remains'. We trust Folio positioning of entrances and exits to a greater degree than most editors.

Editorial Stage Directions such as stage business, asides, indications of addressee and of characters' position on the gallery stage are only used sparingly in Folio. Other editions mingle directions of this kind with original Folio and Quarto directions, sometimes marking them by means of square brackets. We have sought to distinguish what could be described as *directorial* interventions of this kind from Folio-style directions (either original or supplied) by placing them in the right margin in a different typeface. There is a degree of subjectivity about which directions are of which kind, but the procedure is intended as a reminder to the reader and the actor that Shakespearean stage directions are often dependent upon editorial inference alone and are not set in stone. We also depart from editorial tradition in sometimes admitting uncertainty and thus printing permissive stage directions, such as an *Aside?* (often a line may be equally effective as an aside or a direct address – it is for each production or reading to make its own decision) or a *may exit* or a piece of business placed between arrows to indicate that it may occur at various different moments within a scene.

Line Numbers in the left margin are editorial, for reference and to key the explanatory and textual notes.

Explanatory Notes at the foot of each page explain allusions and gloss obsolete and difficult words, confusing phraseology, occasional major textual cruces, and so on. Particular attention is given to non-standard usage, bawdy innuendo and technical terms (e.g. legal and military language). Where more than one sense is given, commas indicate shades of related meaning, slashes alternative or double meanings.

Textual Notes at the end of the play indicate major departures from the Folio. They take the following form: the reading of our text is given in bold and its source given after an equals sign, with 'F2' indicating that it derives from the Second Folio of 1632 and 'Ed' that it derives from the subsequent editorial tradition. The rejected Folio ('F') reading is then given. Thus for Act 1 scene 1 line 142: '**142 eyes** = Q. F = eie' means that the Folio compositor erroneously printed Quarto's 'eyes' as 'eie', and we have restored the Quarto reading.

KEY FACTS

MAJOR PARTS: (*with percentage of lines/number of speeches/scenes on stage*) Bottom (12%/59/5), Theseus(11%/48/3), Helena (11%/36/5), Robin Goodfellow (10%/33/6). Oberon (10%/29/5), Lysander (8%/50/50/5), Hermia (8%/48/5), Titania (7%/23/5), Demetrius (6%/48/5), Quince (5%/40/4), Flute (3%/18/4), Egeus (3%/13/3), Hippolyta (2%/14/3).

LINGUISTIC MEDIUM: 80% verse, 20% prose. Fairly high incidence of rhyme, including deliberately bad rhyme in 'Pyramus and Thisbe'.

DATE: Mentioned in Francis Meres' 1598 list of Shakespeare's plays. Reference in Act 1 scene 2 to courtiers being afraid of a stage lion may allude to an incident in Scotland in August 1594. Strong stylistic resemblances to other 'lyrical' plays of Shakespeare's high Elizabethan period, such as *Richard II* and especially *Romeo and Juliet:* this group of plays is traditionally dated to 1595–96. It has often been speculated that the first performance was a private one at an aristocratic wedding celebration, but there is absolutely no evidence for this: in the Elizabethan period, masque-like entertainments rather than full-length plays were commissioned for festive occasions such as weddings.

SOURCES: The main plot is apparently without a direct source, which is unusual for Shakespeare. The tale of Pyramus and Thisbe is derived principally from Ovid's *Metamorphoses,* book four. It also has strong structural resemblances to the Romeo and Juliet story, which Shakespeare dramatized around the same time. The play as a whole absorbs much of Shakespeare's eclectic reading: numerous borrowings of Ovidian mythology, some use of Sir Thomas North's translation of Plutarch, influence from John Lyly's comedies (especially *Endimion* for dreaming and *Gallathea* for the interplay of aristocrats and artisans), an element of Chaucer (*The Knight's Tale* for lovers at the court of Theseus, perhaps *The Tale of Sir Thopas* for the dream of sleeping with an 'elf-queen'), perhaps *The Golden Ass* of Apuleius (trans, William Adlington, 1566) for Bottom's transformation.

TEXT: Quarto 1600, 'as it hath been sundry times publicly acted by the Right Honourable the Lord Chamberlain his Servants'. apparently typeset from Shakespeare's manuscript or a close transcription of it. Reprinted 1619 (Second Quarto). Folio text was set from a copy of the Second Quarto (thus repeating many of its corrections and errors), but with some consultation of an independent theatre-derived manuscript, which provided additional stage directions, some corrections, and signs of a few revisions, most notably an economizing on roles whereby the Philostrate of Quarto becomes a silent character who only appears in the first scene and the role of Master of the Revels introducing the entertainment in the final scene is taken over by Egeus (which makes for nice tension between him and Lysander, the new son-in-law he did not want). Our edition retains this innovation as well as many local Folio corrections and modernizations, but restores Quarto in many cases where words are mis-set, omitted or transposed as a result of what was almost certainly compositor's error as opposed to editorial alterations on the basis of the theatre manuscript.

A MIDSUMMER NIGHT'S DREAM

THESEUS, Duke of Athens

HIPPOLYTA, Queen of the Amazons, betrothed to Theseus

EGEUS, an Athenian courtier, father to Hermia

LYSANDER, in love with Hermia

HERMIA, in love with Lysander, but ordered by her father to marry Demetrius

DEMETRIUS, in love with Hermia, though once a suitor to Helena

HELENA, in love with Demetrius

Peter QUINCE, a carpenter and leader of an amateur dramatic group, who speaks the PROLOGUE to their play

Nick BOTTOM, a weaver, who plays PYRAMUS in the amateur play

Francis FLUTE, a bellows-mender, who plays THISBE in the amateur play

SNUG, a joiner, who plays a LION in the amateur play

Tom SNOUT, a tinker, who plays a WALL in the amateur play

Robin STARVELING, a tailor, who plays MOONSHINE in the amateur play

OBERON, King of Fairies

TITANIA, Queen of Fairies

ROBIN Goodfellow, also known as Puck, a sprite in the service of Oberon

PEASEBLOSSOM ⎱ fairies
COBWEB ⎰ attendant
MOTH ⎱ upon
MUSTARDSEED ⎰ Titania

PHILOSTRATE, an official in Theseus' court

Other Attendants at the court of Theseus; other Fairies attendant upon Oberon

---

PHILOSTRATE ... court in the Quarto text, he is the Master of the Revels who introduces the entertainment in the final act; in Folio, this role is taken by Egeus, leaving Philostrate a non-speaking role in the first scene.

Act 1 [Scene 1]   *running scene 1*

*Enter Theseus, Hippolyta, with others [Philostrate and
attendants]*

THESEUS Now, fair Hippolyta, our nuptial hour
    Draws on apace. Four happy days bring in
    Another moon: but O, methinks, how slow
    This old moon wanes; she lingers my desires,
5   Like to a stepdame or a dowager
    Long withering out a young man's revenue.
HIPPOLYTA Four days will quickly steep themselves in
      nights,
    Four nights will quickly dream away the time.
    And then the moon, like to a silver bow
10   New-bent in heaven, shall behold the night
    Of our solemnities.
THESEUS Go, Philostrate,
    Stir up the Athenian youth to merriments,
    Awake the pert and nimble spirit of mirth,
15   Turn melancholy forth to funerals:
    The pale companion is not for our pomp.
                            [Exit Philostrate]
    Hippolyta, I wooed thee with my sword,
    And won thy love doing thee injuries.
    But I will wed thee in another key,
20   With pomp, with triumph and with revelling.
*Enter Egeus and his daughter Hermia, Lysander and
Demetrius*
EGEUS Happy be Theseus, our renownèd duke.
THESEUS Thanks, good Egeus: what's the news with thee?
EGEUS Full of vexation come I, with complaint
    Against my child, my daughter Hermia.

1.1 *Location: Athens*   ***Theseus*** mythical Duke of Athens who conquered the Amazons   ***Hippolyta***
mythical Queen of the Amazons, captured by Theseus   **2 apace** quickly   **Four happy days** the action
actually extends over two days and the intervening night   **4 lingers** draws out/keeps waiting   **5 Like to**
like   **stepdame** stepmother   **dowager** widow   **6 withering out** i.e. using up   **young man's revenue**
i.e. her son's inheritance   **7 steep** soak, be suffused in   **9 moon . . . bow** Diana was goddess of hunting and
the moon   **10 New-bent** ready to be strung or to let an arrow loose   **11 solemnities** ceremonies,
celebrations   **14 pert** lively   **16 pale companion** melancholy fellow   **pomp** splendid display, ceremony
17 with my sword Hippolyta was captured during Theseus' campaign against the Amazons   **18 injuries**
wrongs   **20 triumph** public celebration   ***Hermia*** name of Aristotle's disreputable mistress; may be derived
from 'Hermione' (daughter of Helen of Troy)   ***Lysander*** derived from 'Alexander' (another name for Paris,
who carried off Helen of Troy)   ***Demetrius*** a villainous Demetrius appears in North's Plutarch and in
Shakespeare's *Titus Andronicus*

25   Stand forth, Demetrius. My noble lord,
     This man hath my consent to marry her.
     Stand forth, Lysander. And my gracious duke,
     This man hath bewitched the bosom of my child.—
     Thou, thou, Lysander, thou hast given her rhymes,
30   And interchanged love-tokens with my child.
     Thou hast by moonlight at her window sung,
     With feigning voice verses of feigning love,
     And stol'n the impression of her fantasy
     With bracelets of thy hair, rings, gauds, conceits,
35   Knacks, trifles, nosegays, sweetmeats — messengers
     Of strong prevailment in unhardened youth —
     With cunning hast thou filched my daughter's heart,
     Turned her obedience, which is due to me,
     To stubborn harshness.— And, my gracious duke,
40   Be it so she will not here before your grace
     Consent to marry with Demetrius,
     I beg the ancient privilege of Athens:
     As she is mine, I may dispose of her;
     Which shall be either to this gentleman
45   Or to her death, according to our law
     Immediately provided in that case.
     THESEUS What say you, Hermia? Be advised, fair maid,
     To you your father should be as a god,
     One that composed your beauties, yea, and one
50   To whom you are but as a form in wax
     By him imprinted and within his power
     To leave the figure or disfigure it.
     Demetrius is a worthy gentleman.
     HERMIA So is Lysander.
55   THESEUS In himself he is.
     But in this kind, wanting your father's voice,
     The other must be held the worthier.
     HERMIA I would my father looked but with my eyes.
     THESEUS Rather your eyes must with his judgement look.
60   HERMIA I do entreat your grace to pardon me.
     I know not by what power I am made bold,
     Nor how it may concern my modesty

32 feigning singing softly/deceitful/joyful/desirous/longing   33 stol'n ... fantasy cunningly imprinted
yourself in her imagination   34 gauds showy playthings   conceits trinkets   35 knacks knick-knacks
trifles insignificant tokens   nosegays small bouquets of flowers   sweetmeats confectionery
36 prevailment persuasion, influence   unhardened inexperienced, yielding   37 filched stolen   40 Be it
so if   46 Immediately directly   52 disfigure alter/erase   56 kind respect   wanting lacking   voice
approval   58 would wish   62 concern befit

In such a presence here to plead my thoughts:
But I beseech your grace that I may know
65 The worst that may befall me in this case,
If I refuse to wed Demetrius.

THESEUS Either to die the death or to abjure
Forever the society of men.
Therefore, fair Hermia, question your desires,
70 Know of your youth, examine well your blood,
Whether, if you yield not to your father's choice,
You can endure the livery of a nun,
For aye to be in shady cloister mewed,
To live a barren sister all your life,
75 Chanting faint hymns to the cold fruitless moon.
Thrice blessèd they that master so their blood,
To undergo such maiden pilgrimage.
But earthlier happy is the rose distilled
Than that which withering on the virgin thorn
80 Grows, lives and dies in single blessedness.

HERMIA So will I grow, so live, so die, my lord,
Ere I will yield my virgin patent up
Unto his lordship, whose unwishèd yoke
My soul consents not to give sovereignty.

85 **THESEUS** Take time to pause, and by the next new
        moon —
The sealing day betwixt my love and me,
For everlasting bond of fellowship —
Upon that day either prepare to die
For disobedience to your father's will,
90 Or else to wed Demetrius, as he would,
Or on Diana's altar to protest
For aye austerity and single life.

DEMETRIUS Relent, sweet Hermia.— And, Lysander, yield
Thy crazèd title to my certain right.

95 **LYSANDER** You have her father's love, Demetrius:
Let me have Hermia's. Do you marry him.

EGEUS Scornful Lysander! True, he hath my love;
And what is mine my love shall render him.

---

63 presence the duke/assembled people/ceremonial place   **67 die the death** be executed   **68 society** company   **70 Know of** learn from   **blood** passions   **72 livery** clothing (and lifestyle)   **73 aye** always   **mewed** confined   **78 earthlier happy** i.e. more happy on earth   **distilled** whose essence is extracted for perfume   **80 single blessedness** i.e. celibacy   **82 Ere** before   **virgin patent** privilege of virginity   **83 his lordship** i.e. Demetrius   **86 sealing day** i.e. wedding day   **90 would** wishes   **91 Diana** Roman goddess of chastity and the moon   **protest** vow   **92 aye** ever   **94 crazèd** flawed/unsound/mad   **title** claim   **96 Do** i.e. why don't   **98 render** give to

And she is mine, and all my right of her
100   I do estate unto Demetrius.
LYSANDER I am, my lord, as well derived as he,
      As well possessed: my love is more than his,
      My fortunes every way as fairly ranked,
      If not with vantage, as Demetrius',
105   And, which is more than all these boasts can be,
      I am beloved of beauteous Hermia.
      Why should not I then prosecute my right?
      Demetrius, I'll avouch it to his head,
      Made love to Nedar's daughter, Helena,
110   And won her soul: and she, sweet lady, dotes,
      Devoutly dotes, dotes in idolatry,
      Upon this spotted and inconstant man.
THESEUS I must confess that I have heard so much,
      And with Demetrius thought to have spoke thereof,
115   But, being over-full of self-affairs,
      My mind did lose it. But, Demetrius, come,
      And come, Egeus, you shall go with me.
      I have some private schooling for you both.
      For you, fair Hermia, look you arm yourself
120   To fit your fancies to your father's will,
      Or else the law of Athens yields you up —
      Which by no means we may extenuate —
      To death or to a vow of single life.—
      Come, my Hippolyta. What cheer, my love?—
125   Demetrius and Egeus, go along:
      I must employ you in some business
      Against our nuptial and confer with you
      Of something nearly that concerns yourselves.
EGEUS With duty and desire we follow you.
                    Exeunt all but Lysander and Hermia
130 **LYSANDER** How now, my love! Why is your cheek so pale?
      How chance the roses there do fade so fast?
HERMIA Belike for want of rain, which I could well
      Beteem them from the tempest of mine eyes.
LYSANDER Ay me, for aught that I could ever read,
135   Could ever hear by tale or history,

100 estate unto bestow upon   **101 derived** descended   **102 possessed** propertied, i.e. affluent
103 fairly nobly/equally   **104 with … Demetrius'** superior to those of Demetrius   **107 prosecute** pursue
108 avouch declare   **head** i.e. face   **109 Made love to** wooed   **Helena** perhaps named after Helen of
Troy   **110 dotes** is infatuated   **112 spotted** (morally) stained   **115 self-affairs** personal matters
116 lose forget   **118 schooling** admonition/advice   **119 look** be sure   **arm** prepare   **120 fancies**
desires   **122 extenuate** moderate   **125 go** come   **127 Against** in preparation for   **128 nearly that** that
closely   **132 Belike** probably   **133 Beteem** grant   **134 aught** anything, whatever

The course of true love never did run smooth.
But either it was different in blood—
HERMIA O cross! Too high to be enthralled to low.
LYSANDER Or else misgraffèd in respect of years—
140   **HERMIA** O spite! Too old to be engaged to young.
LYSANDER Or else it stood upon the choice of merit—
HERMIA O hell! To choose love by another's eyes.
LYSANDER Or if there were a sympathy in choice,
   War, death or sickness did lay siege to it,
145   Making it momentary as a sound,
   Swift as a shadow, short as any dream:
   Brief as the lightning in the collied night,
   That in a spleen unfolds both heaven and earth,
   And ere a man hath power to say 'Behold!'
150   The jaws of darkness do devour it up:
   So quick bright things come to confusion.
HERMIA If then true lovers have been ever crossed,
   It stands as an edict in destiny.
   Then let us teach our trial patience,
155   Because it is a customary cross,
   As due to love as thoughts and dreams and sighs,
   Wishes and tears, poor fancy's followers.
LYSANDER A good persuasion. Therefore hear me,
   Hermia.
   I have a widow aunt, a dowager
160   Of great revenue, and she hath no child.
   From Athens is her house removed seven leagues,
   And she respects me as her only son.
   There, gentle Hermia, may I marry thee,
   And to that place the sharp Athenian law
165   Cannot pursue us. If thou lov'st me, then
   Steal forth thy father's house tomorrow night,
   And in the wood, a league without the town,
   Where I did meet thee once with Helena,
   To do observance to a morn of May,
170   There will I stay for thee.

---

137 blood rank   **138 cross** hindrance/vexation   **139 misgraffèd** mismatched   **141 stood** depended
merit Folio's emendation of Quarto's 'friends' (meaning 'relatives'); some editors assume that both texts are
wrong and that the line should read 'Or merit stood upon the choice of friends'   **143 sympathy** agreement
145 momentary fleeting   **147 collied** blackened   **148 spleen** fit of temper   **unfolds** reveals   **149 ere**
before   **151 quick** living/brief   **confusion** ruin   **152 ever crossed** always thwarted   **154 trial**
experience of this trial   **157 fancy's** love's   **158 persuasion** opinion   **161 seven leagues** about twenty-
one miles   **162 respects** considers   **167 without** outside   **169 do … May** i.e. celebrate May Day
170 stay wait

HERMIA My good Lysander!

I swear to thee, by Cupid's strongest bow,

By his best arrow with the golden head,

By the simplicity of Venus' doves,

175 By that which knitteth souls and prospers love,

And by that fire which burned the Carthage queen,

When the false Troyan under sail was seen,

By all the vows that ever men have broke,

In number more than ever women spoke,

180 In that same place thou hast appointed me,

Tomorrow truly will I meet with thee.

LYSANDER Keep promise, love. Look, here comes Helena.

Enter Helena

HERMIA God speed fair Helena, whither away?

HELENA Call you me fair? That fair again unsay.

185 Demetrius loves your fair: O happy fair!

Your eyes are lodestars, and your tongue's sweet air

More tuneable than lark to shepherd's ear

When wheat is green, when hawthorn buds appear.

Sickness is catching: O, were favour so,

190 Your words I catch, fair Hermia, ere I go,

My ear should catch your voice, my eye your eye,

My tongue should catch your tongue's sweet melody.

Were the world mine, Demetrius being bated,

The rest I'll give to be to you translated.

195 O, teach me how you look, and with what art

You sway the motion of Demetrius' heart.

HERMIA I frown upon him, yet he loves me still.

HELENA O, that your frowns would teach my smiles
such skill!

HERMIA I give him curses, yet he gives me love.

200 **HELENA** O, that my prayers could such affection move!

HERMIA The more I hate, the more he follows me.

HELENA The more I love, the more he hateth me.

HERMIA His folly, Helena, is none of mine.

HELENA None, but your beauty: would that fault were
mine!

---

172 **Cupid** Roman god of love   173 **best . . . head** i.e. one causing love (Cupid's lead arrows were supposed to induce loathing)   174 **simplicity** innocence   **doves** symbols of fidelity, these birds drew the goddess of love's chariot   175 **knitteth** binds together   176 **Carthage queen** Dido, who committed suicide on a pyre when Aeneas deserted her   177 **false Troyan** the Trojan Aeneas   183 **fair** beautiful/fair-complexioned   185 **happy** favoured, lucky   186 **lodestars** guiding stars   **air** melody   187 **tuneable** harmonious   188 **green** fresh, new   189 **favour** good looks/a favourable attitude   190 **catch** seize   193 **bated** omitted (with play on 'baited, hooked')   194 **translated** transformed   200 **move** arouse   203 **none** i.e. no fault

205 HERMIA Take comfort: he no more shall see my face.
      Lysander and myself will fly this place.
      Before the time I did Lysander see,
      Seemed Athens like a paradise to me.
      O, then, what graces in my love do dwell,
210   That he hath turned a heaven into hell!
    LYSANDER Helen, to you our minds we will unfold:
      Tomorrow night, when Phoebe doth behold
      Her silver visage in the wat'ry glass,
      Decking with liquid pearl the bladed grass,
215   A time that lovers' flights doth still conceal,
      Through Athens' gates have we devised to steal.
    HERMIA And in the wood, where often you and I
      Upon faint primrose beds were wont to lie,
      Emptying our bosoms of their counsel sweet,
220   There my Lysander and myself shall meet,
      And thence from Athens turn away our eyes,
      To seek new friends and strange companions.
      Farewell, sweet playfellow: pray thou for us,
      And good luck grant thee thy Demetrius! —
225   Keep word, Lysander: we must starve our sight
      From lovers' food till morrow deep midnight.   *Exit*
    LYSANDER I will, my Hermia.— Helena, adieu.
      As you on him, Demetrius dote on you!   *Exit*
    HELENA How happy some o'er other some can be!
230   Through Athens I am thought as fair as she.
      But what of that? Demetrius thinks not so:
      He will not know what all but he doth know.
      And as he errs, doting on Hermia's eyes,
      So I, admiring of his qualities.
235   Things base and vile, holding no quantity,
      Love can transpose to form and dignity.
      Love looks not with the eyes, but with the mind,
      And therefore is winged Cupid painted blind.
      Nor hath love's mind of any judgement taste,
240   Wings and no eyes figure unheedy haste.
      And therefore is love said to be a child,
      Because in choice he is often beguiled.

---

206 fly flee   212 Phoebe another name for the Roman moon goddess   213 glass mirror (i.e. water)
215 still always   218 faint pale   wont accustomed   219 counsel inmost thoughts/advice   222 strange
foreign, new   229 o'er other some more than others   232 all everyone else   235 quantity value/
substance/proportion (to what love makes them into)   236 form ordered, attractive appearance/substance
238 blind Cupid was traditionally depicted as a sightless child   239 of ... taste the least bit of reason
240 figure symbolize   242 beguiled deceived, misguided

As waggish boys in game themselves forswear,
So the boy love is perjured everywhere.
245 For ere Demetrius looked on Hermia's eyne,
He hailed down oaths that he was only mine.
And when this hail some heat from Hermia felt,
So he dissolved, and showers of oaths did melt.
I will go tell him of fair Hermia's flight:
250 Then to the wood will he tomorrow night
Pursue her; and for this intelligence,
If I have thanks, it is a dear expense.
But herein mean I to enrich my pain,
To have his sight thither and back again.   *Exit*

[Act 1 Scene 2]   *running scene 2*

*Enter Quince the carpenter, Snug the joiner, Bottom the
weaver, Flute the bellows-mender, Snout the tinker and
Starveling the tailor*

QUINCE Is all our company here?
BOTTOM You were best to call them generally, man by
    man, according to the scrip.
QUINCE Here is the scroll of every man's name, which is
5   thought fit through all Athens to play in our
    interlude before the duke and the duchess on his
    wedding day at night.
BOTTOM First, good Peter Quince, say what the play
    treats on, then read the names of the actors, and so
10   grow on to a point.
QUINCE Marry, our play is 'The most lamentable comedy
    and most cruel death of Pyramus and Thisbe.'
BOTTOM A very good piece of work, I assure you, and a
    merry. Now, good Peter Quince, call forth your
15   actors by the scroll. Masters, spread yourselves.
QUINCE Answer as I call you. Nick Bottom, the weaver.

243 **waggish** playful, mischievous **game** jest/play **themselves forswear** break their word 245 **eyne** eyes 251 **intelligence** information 252 **dear expense** effort worth making/high price to pay (as Demetrius will pursue Hermia)/begrudging gratitude (from Demetrius) 1.2 *Quince* probably from 'quines' or 'quoins', a **carpenter's** wooden wedges *Snug* close-fitting; a good name for a **joiner** (craftsman who makes furniture) *Bottom* the core onto which the **weaver's** yarn was wound, or a ball of thread; did not have modern sense of 'arse' *Flute* suggests the fluted pipes of a church-organ operated by **bellows**; perhaps Flute also has a reedy, high voice *Snout* possibly Snout has a large nose (some editors suppose a reference to the spout of a kettle, which a **tinker** would have to mend, but sixteenth-century kettles did not have spouts) *Starveling* tailors were proverbially thin 2 **generally** malapropism for 'severally' (i.e. individually) 3 **scrip** scrap of paper/script (i.e. what is written down; the word did not have its modern theatrical sense) 6 **interlude** short play 9 **treats on** deals with, is about 10 **grow ... point** approach a conclusion 11 **Marry** by the Virgin Mary 15 **spread yourselves** spread out

BOTTOM Ready. Name what part I am for, and proceed.

QUINCE You, Nick Bottom, are set down for Pyramus.

BOTTOM What is Pyramus, a lover or a tyrant?

20 **QUINCE** A lover that kills himself most gallantly for love.

BOTTOM That will ask some tears in the true performing
of it. If I do it, let the audience look to their eyes: I will
move storms; I will condole in some measure. To the
rest — yet my chief humour is for a tyrant: I could
25 play Ercles rarely, or a part to tear a cat in, to make
all split.

> The raging rocks
> And shivering shocks
> Shall break the locks
30 > Of prison gates.
> And Phibbus' car
> Shall shine from far
> And make and mar
> The foolish Fates.

35 This was lofty. Now name the rest of the players. This
is Ercles' vein, a tyrant's vein: a lover is more
condoling.

QUINCE Francis Flute, the bellows-mender.

FLUTE Here, Peter Quince.

40 **QUINCE** You must take Thisbe on you.

FLUTE What is Thisbe? A wand'ring knight?

QUINCE It is the lady that Pyramus must love.

FLUTE Nay, faith, let not me play a woman: I have a
beard coming.

45 **QUINCE** That's all one. You shall play it in a mask, and
you may speak as small as you will.

BOTTOM An I may hide my face, let me play Thisbe too.
I'll speak in a monstrous little voice. 'Thisne, Thisne!'
'Ah, Pyramus, my lover dear! Thy Thisbe dear and
50 lady dear!'

QUINCE No, no, you must play Pyramus.— And, Flute,
you Thisbe.

BOTTOM Well, proceed.

QUINCE Robin Starveling, the tailor.

---

21 **ask** require   23 **condole** express great sorrow   24 **humour** inclination   25 **Ercles** i.e. the Greek hero
Hercules   **rarely** magnificently, exceptionally   **tear ... in** rant and bluster   26 **split** go to pieces
28 **shivering** shattering   31 **Phibbus' car** the chariot of Phoebus, the sun god   33 **mar** ruin   34 **Fates**
three goddesses in control of human destiny   35 **lofty** grandiose, exalted, impressive   36 **vein**
temperament   41 **wand'ring** i.e. on a mission   45 **That's all one** it doesn't matter   46 **small** high-pitched
will can   47 **An** if

55   **STARVELING** Here, Peter Quince.

QUINCE Robin Starveling, you must play Thisbe's mother. Tom Snout, the tinker.

SNOUT Here, Peter Quince.

QUINCE You, Pyramus' father; myself, Thisbe's father;
60   Snug the joiner, you, the lion's part: and I hope there is a play fitted.

SNUG Have you the lion's part written? Pray you, if it be, give it me, for I am slow of study.

QUINCE You may do it extempore, for it is nothing but
65   roaring.

BOTTOM Let me play the lion too: I will roar that I will do any man's heart good to hear me. I will roar that I will make the duke say 'Let him roar again, let him roar again.'

70   **QUINCE** If you should do it too terribly, you would fright the duchess and the ladies that they would shriek, and that were enough to hang us all.

ALL That would hang us, every mother's son.

BOTTOM I grant you, friends, if that you should fright the
75   ladies out of their wits, they would have no more discretion but to hang us: but I will aggravate my voice so that I will roar you as gently as any sucking dove. I will roar an 'twere any nightingale.

QUINCE You can play no part but Pyramus, for Pyramus
80   is a sweet-faced man, a proper man, as one shall see in a summer's day; a most lovely gentlemanlike man: therefore you must needs play Pyramus.

BOTTOM Well, I will undertake it. What beard were I best to play it in?

85   **QUINCE** Why, what you will.

BOTTOM I will discharge it in either your straw-colour beard, your orange-tawny beard, your purple-in-grain beard, or your French-crown-coloured beard, your perfect yellow.

90   **QUINCE** Some of your French crowns have no hair at all, and then you will play bare-faced. But, masters, here *Passes out*
are your parts: and I am to entreat you, request you *the parts*

56 **Thisbe's … father** these characters never actually appear   61 **fitted** equipped, provided for (perhaps maintaining the language of joinery)   64 **do it extempore** improvise   76 **discretion** sound judgement **aggravate** malapropism for 'moderate'   77 **roar** roar for   **sucking dove** conflation of 'sitting dove' and 'sucking lamb', both proverbially quiet and gentle   78 **an 'twere** as if it were   80 **proper** handsome 86 **discharge** perform   **your** i.e. you know the sort   87 **orange-tawny** yellowish-brown   **purple-in-grain** dyed red   88 **French-crown-coloured** i.e. the gold colour of the French coin   90 **crowns** heads; baldness was an effect of syphilis ('the French disease')

and desire you, to con them by tomorrow night, and
meet me in the palace wood a mile without the town
95   by moonlight. There will we rehearse, for if we meet
in the city we shall be dogged with company, and our
devices known. In the meantime I will draw a bill of
properties, such as our play wants. I pray you fail
me not.

100   BOTTOM We will meet, and there we may rehearse more
obscenely and courageously. Take pains, be perfect.
Adieu.

QUINCE At the duke's oak we meet.

BOTTOM Enough. Hold or cut bow-strings.   *Exeunt*

Act 2 [Scene 1]   *running scene 3*

*Enter a Fairy at one door and Robin Goodfellow [Puck]
at another*

ROBIN How now, spirit, whither wander you?

FAIRY   Over hill, over dale,
         Through bush, through brier,
         Over park, over pale,
5   Thorough flood, thorough fire,
         I do wander everywhere,
         Swifter than the moon's sphere;
         And I serve the fairy queen,
         To dew her orbs upon the green.
10   The cowslips tall her pensioners be,
         In their gold coats spots you see,
         Those be rubies, fairy favours,
         In those freckles live their savours.
         I must go seek some dewdrops here,
15   And hang a pearl in every cowslip's ear.
      Farewell, thou lob of spirits, I'll be gone:
      Our queen and all her elves come here anon.

ROBIN The king doth keep his revels here tonight:
      Take heed the queen come not within his sight,

93 con learn   97 devices plans   draw draw up   bill list   101 obscenely malapropism, perhaps for
'seemly' or 'obscurely' (secretly)   courageously spiritedly   perfect word perfect   104 hold ... bow-
strings archers' saying, possibly meaning 'stand firm and fight, or cut your bow-strings in preparation for
capture'   2.1   *Location: a wood near Athens*   *Robin Goodfellow* name traditionally given to a
mischievous hobgoblin   *Puck* a kind of mischievous spirit or goblin   4 park enclosed hunting ground
pale fenced-in area   5 Thorough through   7 sphere orbit; stars and planets were thought to be contained
within revolving hollow spheres   9 orbs i.e. fairy rings (dark circles in the grass)   10 pensioners
bodyguards   12 favours tokens of favour   13 savours (sweet) scent   16 lob country bumpkin   17 anon
soon

20   For Oberon is passing fell and wrath,
     Because that she as her attendant hath
     A lovely boy, stol'n from an Indian king.
     She never had so sweet a changeling,
     And jealous Oberon would have the child
25   Knight of his train, to trace the forests wild.
     But she perforce withholds the lovèd boy,
     Crowns him with flowers and makes him all her joy.
     And now they never meet in grove or green,
     By fountain clear or spangled starlight sheen,
30   But they do square, that all their elves for fear
     Creep into acorn cups and hide them there.
FAIRY   Either I mistake your shape and making quite,
     Or else you are that shrewd and knavish sprite
     Called Robin Goodfellow. Are not you he
35   That frights the maidens of the villagery,
     Skim milk, and sometimes labour in the quern,
     And bootless make the breathless housewife churn,
     And sometime make the drink to bear no barm,
     Mislead night-wanderers, laughing at their harm?
40   Those that Hobgoblin call you and sweet Puck,
     You do their work and they shall have good luck.
     Are not you he?
ROBIN   Thou speak'st aright;
     I am that merry wanderer of the night.
45   I jest to Oberon and make him smile
     When I a fat and bean-fed horse beguile,
     Neighing in likeness of a filly foal,
     And sometime lurk I in a gossip's bowl,
     In very likeness of a roasted crab,
50   And when she drinks, against her lips I bob
     And on her withered dewlap pour the ale.
     The wisest aunt, telling the saddest tale,
     Sometime for three-foot stool mistaketh me,
     Then slip I from her bum, down topples she,
55   And 'tailor' cries, and falls into a cough.

20 **passing fell** excessively fierce   **wrath** angry   23 **changeling** child taken by the fairies (usually exchanged for a fairy child)   25 **trace** traverse   26 **perforce** forcibly   29 **fountain** spring   **sheen** brightness   30 **square** quarrel   32 **making** physical appearance   **quite** entirely   33 **shrewd** cunning 35 **villagery** villages   36 **Skim** take the cream off   **quern** churn; also a mill for grinding corn 37 **bootless** in vain   38 **barm** yeasty froth on top of fermenting ale   39 **mislead** i.e. with false fire that moves from place to place   46 **bean-fed** well-fed   47 **filly** female   48 **gossip's** old friend's   **bowl** i.e. drinking cup   49 **crab** crab-apple   51 **dewlap** loose fold of skin hanging at the neck   52 **aunt** old woman   55 **'tailor'** cry of surprise; possibly because she ends up sitting on the floor (customary posture for tailors), or because she sits on her 'tail' (i.e. **bum**)

And then the whole quire hold their hips and laugh,
And waxen in their mirth and neeze and swear
A merrier hour was never wasted there.
But, room, fairy! Here comes Oberon.

60 **FAIRY** And here my mistress. Would that he were gone!
Enter the King of Fairies [Oberon] at one door with his train,
and the Queen [Titania] at another with hers
OBERON Ill met by moonlight, proud Titania.
TITANIA What, jealous Oberon? Fairies, skip hence.
I have forsworn his bed and company.
OBERON Tarry, rash wanton, am not I thy lord?

65 **TITANIA** Then I must be thy lady: but I know
When thou hast stol'n away from fairy land,
And in the shape of Corin sat all day,
Playing on pipes of corn and versing love
To amorous Phillida. Why art thou here,

70 Come from the farthest step of India?
But that, forsooth, the bouncing Amazon,
Your buskined mistress and your warrior love,
To Theseus must be wedded; and you come
To give their bed joy and prosperity?

75 **OBERON** How canst thou thus for shame, Titania,
Glance at my credit with Hippolyta,
Knowing I know thy love to Theseus?
Didst not thou lead him through the glimmering night
From Perigenia whom he ravishèd?

80 And make him with fair Aegles break his faith,
With Ariadne and Antiopa?

TITANIA These are the forgeries of jealousy,
And never since the middle summer's spring
Met we on hill, in dale, forest or mead,

85 By pavèd fountain or by rushy brook,
Or in the beachèd margent of the sea,

---

56 quire company   **57 waxen** increase   **neeze** sneeze   **58 wasted** spent   **59 room** make way
Oberon name often given to the King of Fairies   ***Titania*** used by Ovid to refer to Diana (moon goddess) and
Circe (enchantress)   **64 Tarry** stay   **wanton** wilful one, perhaps also with sense of 'promiscuous'   **lord**
husband   **65 lady** wife   **67 Corin** conventional pastoral name   **68 corn** straw   **versing** composing/
uttering verses of   **69 Phillida** conventional pastoral name   **70 step** limit   **71 forsooth** in truth
bouncing big, strapping (perhaps with sexual connotations)   **72 buskined** wearing high hunting boots
('buskins')   **76 Glance at** refer to/cast aspersions on   **credit** favour   **78 glimmering** twinkling,
shimmering   **79 Perigenia** (sometimes spelt 'Perigouna') Theseus slept with her after he killed her robber
father   **ravishèd** carried off/seized/raped   **80 Aegles** nymph loved by Theseus   **81 Ariadne** she helped
Theseus find his way out of the Cretan labyrinth; he then abandoned her   **Antiopa** Amazon seduced or
abducted by Theseus before being abandoned by him   **83 middle summer's spring** i.e. beginning of
midsummer   **84 mead** meadow   **85 pavèd** with a pebbly base   **rushy** edged with rushes   **86 in** on
beachèd covered with shingle   **margent** margin, edge

To dance our ringlets to the whistling wind,
But with thy brawls thou hast disturbed our sport.
Therefore the winds, piping to us in vain,
90 As in revenge, have sucked up from the sea
Contagious fogs, which falling in the land
Hath every petty river made so proud
That they have overborne their continents.
The ox hath therefore stretched his yoke in vain,
95 The ploughman lost his sweat, and the green corn
Hath rotted ere his youth attained a beard.
The fold stands empty in the drownèd field,
And crows are fatted with the murrion flock,
The nine men's morris is filled up with mud,
100 And the quaint mazes in the wanton green
For lack of tread are undistinguishable.
The human mortals want their winter here:
No night is now with hymn or carol blessed.
Therefore the moon, the governess of floods,
105 Pale in her anger, washes all the air,
That rheumatic diseases do abound.
And through this distemperature we see
The seasons alter; hoary-headed frosts
Fall in the fresh lap of the crimson rose,
110 And on old Hiems' thin and icy crown
An odorous chaplet of sweet summer buds
Is, as in mockery, set. The spring, the summer,
The childing autumn, angry winter, change
Their wonted liveries, and the mazèd world
115 By their increase now knows not which is which;
And this same progeny of evils comes
From our debate, from our dissension:
We are their parents and original.

---

87 **ringlets** circular fairy dance   88 **brawls** quarrels/noise; also lively French dance (contrasts with calmer ringlets)   **sport** recreation   89 **piping** whistling   91 **Contagious** pestilential/harmful   92 **petty** small **proud** swollen   93 **overborne their continents** exceeded their boundaries (i.e. flooded)   94 **stretched** strained at/pulled   95 **lost** wasted   96 **ere ... beard** before developing the awn (bristly growth) 97 **fold** animal pen   98 **murrion** infected   99 **nine men's morris** ground marked out for a game involving nine pegs ('men')   100 **quaint** elaborate   **mazes** pattern of paths cut in the turf   **wanton green** lush grass   102 **want ... blessed** i.e. though the weather is wintry, there are no winter festivities (some editors emend 'here' to 'cheer')   104 **Therefore** i.e. because of our dispute   **floods** tides   105 **washes** saturates, renders moist   106 **rheumatic diseases** illnesses involving watery discharge, such as colds 107 **distemperature** poor weather/disorder   108 **hoary-headed** white-haired   110 **Hiems** personification of winter   111 **chaplet** garland   113 **childing** fertile   114 **wonted** customary   **mazèd** confused/ dumbstruck/terrified   115 **increase** produce   117 **debate** discord   **dissension** discord   118 **original** point of origin

OBERON Do you amend it then, it lies in you.
120   Why should Titania cross her Oberon?
       I do but beg a little changeling boy
       To be my henchman.
TITANIA Set your heart at rest:
       The fairy land buys not the child of me.
125   His mother was a votress of my order,
       And in the spicèd Indian air by night
       Full often hath she gossiped by my side,
       And sat with me on Neptune's yellow sands,
       Marking th'embarkèd traders on the flood,
130   When we have laughed to see the sails conceive
       And grow big-bellied with the wanton wind,
       Which she, with pretty and with swimming gait
       Following — her womb then rich with my young
          squire —
       Would imitate, and sail upon the land,
135   To fetch me trifles, and return again
       As from a voyage, rich with merchandise.
       But she, being mortal, of that boy did die:
       And for her sake do I rear up her boy,
       And for her sake I will not part with him.
140 **OBERON** How long within this wood intend you stay?
TITANIA Perchance till after Theseus' wedding day.
       If you will patiently dance in our round
       And see our moonlight revels, go with us;
       If not, shun me, and I will spare your haunts.
145 **OBERON** Give me that boy, and I will go with thee.
TITANIA Not for thy fairy kingdom. Fairies, away.
       We shall chide downright, if I longer stay.
                          Exeunt [*Titania and her train*]
OBERON Well, go thy way: thou shalt not from this grove
       Till I torment thee for this injury.
150   My gentle Puck, come hither. Thou rememb'rest
       Since once I sat upon a promontory,
       And heard a mermaid on a dolphin's back
       Uttering such dulcet and harmonious breath
       That the rude sea grew civil at her song,

122 **henchman** squire, page   125 **votress** female follower, bound by a vow   127 **Full** very
128 **Neptune** Roman god of the sea   129 **Marking** observing, noting   **th'embarkèd traders** sailing
merchants or their ships   **flood** sea   131 **wanton** playful/lustful   132 **swimming gait** smooth, graceful
motion   137 **of that boy** i.e. in childbirth   141 **Perchance** perhaps   142 **patiently** calmly   **round**
circular dance   144 **spare** avoid   147 **chide** quarrel   **downright** utterly   148 **from** go from   151 **Since**
when   **promontory** headland   153 **dulcet** sweet   **breath** i.e. song   154 **rude** rough

155   And certain stars shot madly from their spheres
      To hear the sea-maid's music.
    ROBIN I remember.
    OBERON That very time I saw, but thou couldst not,
      Flying between the cold moon and the earth,
160   Cupid all armed; a certain aim he took
      At a fair vestal thronèd by the west,
      And loosed his love-shaft smartly from his bow,
      As it should pierce a hundred thousand hearts.
      But I might see young Cupid's fiery shaft
165   Quenched in the chaste beams of the wat'ry moon;
      And the imperial votress passèd on,
      In maiden meditation, fancy-free.
      Yet marked I where the bolt of Cupid fell.
      It fell upon a little western flower,
170   Before milk-white, now purple with love's wound,
      And maidens call it love-in-idleness.
      Fetch me that flower; the herb I showed thee once:
      The juice of it on sleeping eyelids laid
      Will make or man or woman madly dote
175   Upon the next live creature that it sees.
      Fetch me this herb, and be thou here again
      Ere the leviathan can swim a league.
    ROBIN I'll put a girdle round about the earth
      In forty minutes.   *[Exit]*
180   **OBERON** Having once this juice,
      I'll watch Titania when she is asleep,
      And drop the liquor of it in her eyes.
      The next thing when she waking looks upon,
      Be it on lion, bear, or wolf or bull,
185   On meddling monkey or on busy ape,
      She shall pursue it with the soul of love.
      And ere I take this charm off from her sight,
      As I can take it with another herb,
      I'll make her render up her page to me.
190   But who comes here? I am invisible,
      And I will overhear their conference.   *He stands aside*
    Enter Demetrius, Helena following him

---

155 certain surely/particular **160 all** fully **certain** accurate/specific **161 vestal** woman vowed to chastity, here assumed by most commentators to be an allusion to Queen Elizabeth I (**the imperial votress**) **163 As** as if **164 might** could **167 fancy-free** unaffected by love **168 bolt** arrow **170 purple** blood-coloured **171 love-in-idleness** pansy or heartsease **174 or** either **177 leviathan** sea monster **178 girdle** belt

DEMETRIUS I love thee not, therefore pursue me not.
Where is Lysander and fair Hermia?
The one I'll stay, the other stayeth me.
195 Thou told'st me they were stolen into this wood;
And here am I, and wood within this wood,
Because I cannot meet my Hermia.
Hence, get thee gone, and follow me no more.
HELENA You draw me, you hard-hearted adamant;
200 But yet you draw not iron, for my heart
Is true as steel. Leave you your power to draw,
And I shall have no power to follow you.
DEMETRIUS Do I entice you? Do I speak you fair?
Or rather do I not in plainest truth
205 Tell you I do not nor I cannot love you?
HELENA And even for that do I love thee the more.
I am your spaniel, and, Demetrius,
The more you beat me, I will fawn on you.
Use me but as your spaniel: spurn me, strike me,
210 Neglect me, lose me; only give me leave,
Unworthy as I am, to follow you.
What worser place can I beg in your love —
And yet a place of high respect with me —
Than to be used as you do use your dog?
215 **DEMETRIUS** Tempt not too much the hatred of my spirit,
For I am sick when I do look on thee.
HELENA And I am sick when I look not on you.
DEMETRIUS You do impeach your modesty too much,
To leave the city and commit yourself
220 Into the hands of one that loves you not,
To trust the opportunity of night
And the ill counsel of a desert place
With the rich worth of your virginity.
HELENA Your virtue is my privilege: for that
225 It is not night when I do see your face,
Therefore I think I am not in the night.
Nor doth this wood lack worlds of company,
For you in my respect are all the world.
Then how can it be said I am alone,
230 When all the world is here to look on me?

---

194 The ... stayeth i.e. I will confront Lysander; it is Hermia who is preoccupying me (some editors emend to 'slay ... slayeth') **196 wood** angry/mad (puns on 'wooed') **199 draw** attract (magnetically) **adamant** hard magnetic substance **201 Leave you** give up **203 you fair** favourably, kindly to you **209 but** only **210 leave** permission **218 impeach** discredit **222 desert** desolate, isolated **224 privilege** safeguard **for that** because

DEMETRIUS I'll run from thee and hide me in the brakes,
    And leave thee to the mercy of wild beasts.
HELENA The wildest hath not such a heart as you.
    Run when you will, the story shall be changed:
235   Apollo flies, and Daphne holds the chase;
    The dove pursues the griffin, the mild hind
    Makes speed to catch the tiger. Bootless speed,
    When cowardice pursues and valour flies.
DEMETRIUS I will not stay thy questions, let me go;
240   Or if thou follow me, do not believe
    But I shall do thee mischief in the wood.
                            [↓*Exit Demetrius*↓]
HELENA Ay, in the temple, in the town, the field,
    You do me mischief. Fie, Demetrius!
    Your wrongs do set a scandal on my sex:
245   We cannot fight for love, as men may do;
    We should be wooed and were not made to woo.
    I'll follow thee and make a heaven of hell,
    To die upon the hand I love so well.   *Exit*
OBERON Fare thee well, nymph: ere he do leave this grove,
250   Thou shalt fly him and he shall seek thy love.
Enter [Robin] Puck
  Hast thou the flower there? Welcome, wanderer.
ROBIN Ay, there it is.   *Shows the flower*
OBERON I pray thee give it me.
    I know a bank where the wild thyme blows,
255   Where oxlips and the nodding violet grows,
    Quite over-canopied with luscious woodbine,
    With sweet musk-roses and with eglantine:
    There sleeps Titania sometime of the night,
    Lulled in these flowers with dances and delight:
260   And there the snake throws her enamelled skin,
    Weed wide enough to wrap a fairy in.
    And with the juice of this I'll streak her eyes,
    And make her full of hateful fantasies.
    Take thou some of it, and seek through this grove; *Gives him some*
265   A sweet Athenian lady is in love   *juice*
    With a disdainful youth: anoint his eyes,

---

231 brakes bushes   **235 Apollo . . . chase** a reversal of the myth in which Daphne, being chased by Apollo, was spared rape by being turned into a laurel tree   **236 griffin** mythical beast, part-lion, part-eagle   **hind** female deer   **237 bootless** pointless   **239 stay** wait for   **244 set . . . sex** make me behave in a way that disgraces womankind   **248 upon** by/at   **254 blows** blossoms   **255 oxlips** flowers resembling both cowslip and primrose   **256 Quite** completely   **woodbine** honeysuckle   **257 musk-roses** wild climbing roses   **eglantine** sweet-briar, a sweetly scented rose   **258 sometime** at some time or other   **260 throws** sheds   **261 Weed** garment

But do it when the next thing he espies
May be the lady. Thou shalt know the man
By the Athenian garments he hath on.
270   Effect it with some care, that he may prove
More fond on her than she upon her love;
And look thou meet me ere the first cock crow.
ROBIN Fear not, my lord, your servant shall do so.

Exeunt

[Act 2 Scene 2]   *running scene 4*

Enter Queen of Fairies [Titania] with her train

TITANIA Come, now a roundel and a fairy song;
Then, for the third part of a minute, hence:
Some to kill cankers in the musk-rose buds,
Some war with reremice for their leathern wings,
5   To make my small elves coats, and some keep back
The clamorous owl that nightly hoots and wonders
At our quaint spirits. Sing me now asleep,
Then to your offices and let me rest.   *She lies down on a bank*
Fairies sing
FIRST FAIRY You spotted snakes with double tongue,
10   Thorny hedgehogs, be not seen.
              Newts and blind-worms, do no wrong,
              Come not near our fairy queen.
CHORUS   Philomel, with melody
              Sing in our sweet lullaby,
15   Lulla, lulla, lullaby, lulla, lulla, lullaby.
              Never harm,
              Nor spell nor charm,
              Come our lovely lady nigh;
              So, goodnight, with lullaby.
20   SECOND FAIRY Weaving spiders, come not here.
              Hence, you long-legged spinners, hence!
              Beetles black, approach not near;
              Worm nor snail, do no offence.
CHORUS   Philomel, with melody, etc.

271 **fond on** infatuated with   **2.2**   1 **roundel** circular dance   3 **cankers** worms that destroy plants
4 **reremice** bats   **leathern** leathery   7 **quaint** strange/dainty   8 **offices** duties   9 **double** i.e. forked
11 **blind-worms** adders   13 **Philomel** nightingale; Philomela was transformed into a nightingale after
being raped by her brother-in-law   18 **nigh** near   24 **etc.** indicates chorus is to be repeated

25   FIRST FAIRY Hence, away! Now all is well;
         One aloof stand sentinel.
                     She [Titania] sleeps. [Exeunt Fairies]
     Enter Oberon
     OBERON What thou see'st when thou dost wake,   *Squeezes juice*
         Do it for thy true-love take,   *on Titania's eyes*
         Love and languish for his sake.
30   Be it ounce or cat or bear,
         Pard, or boar with bristled hair,
         In thy eye that shall appear
         When thou wak'st, it is thy dear.
         Wake when some vile thing is near.   *[Exit]*
     Enter Lysander and Hermia
35   LYSANDER Fair love, you faint with wand'ring in the wood,
         And to speak troth, I have forgot our way:
         We'll rest us, Hermia, if you think it good,
         And tarry for the comfort of the day.
     HERMIA Be it so, Lysander; find you out a bed,
40   For I upon this bank will rest my head.
     LYSANDER One turf shall serve as pillow for us both:
         One heart, one bed, two bosoms and one troth.
     HERMIA Nay, good Lysander, for my sake, my dear,
         Lie further off yet, do not lie so near.
45   LYSANDER O, take the sense, sweet, of my innocence!
         Love takes the meaning in love's conference.
         I mean that my heart unto yours is knit
         So that but one heart we can make of it.
         Two bosoms interchainèd with an oath,
50   So then two bosoms and a single troth.
         Then by your side no bed-room me deny,
         For lying so, Hermia, I do not lie.
     HERMIA Lysander riddles very prettily.
         Now much beshrew my manners and my pride,
55   If Hermia meant to say Lysander lied.
         But, gentle friend, for love and courtesy
         Lie further off, in human modesty:
         Such separation as may well be said
         Becomes a virtuous bachelor and a maid,

26 **aloof** at a distance   **sentinel** guard   30 **ounce** lynx   31 **Pard** leopard/panther   36 **troth** truth
38 **tarry ... day** wait till the cooler part of the day   42 **troth** pledge (of love)/faith   45 **take the sense** i.e.
interpret correctly   46 **Love ... conference** i.e. love allows lovers to understand one another   52 **lie**
mislead (you) (puns on 'lie down')   53 **prettily** charmingly/cleverly   54 **beshrew** curse   56 **friend** lover
57 **human** polite/courteous   59 **Becomes** befits

60   So far be distant, and good night, sweet friend;
      Thy love ne'er alter till thy sweet life end!
      LYSANDER Amen, amen, to that fair prayer, say I,
      And then end life when I end loyalty!
      Here is my bed: sleep give thee all his rest!
65   HERMIA With half that wish the wisher's eyes be pressed!
                                                They sleep

      Enter [Robin] Puck
      ROBIN Through the forest have I gone,
      But Athenian found I none
      On whose eyes I might approve
      This flower's force in stirring love.
70   Night and silence — who is here?   *Sees Lysander*
      Weeds of Athens he doth wear:
      This is he, my master said,
      Despisèd the Athenian maid:
      And here the maiden, sleeping sound,
75   On the dank and dirty ground.
      Pretty soul, she durst not lie
      Near this lack-love, this kill-courtesy.
      Churl, upon thy eyes I throw   *Puts juice on Lysander's eyes*
      All the power this charm doth owe.
80   When thou wak'st, let love forbid
      Sleep his seat on thy eyelid.
      So awake when I am gone,
      For I must now to Oberon.   *Exit*
      Enter Demetrius and Helena, running
      HELENA Stay, though thou kill me, sweet Demetrius.
85   DEMETRIUS I charge thee, hence, and do not haunt
           me thus.
      HELENA O, wilt thou darkling leave me? Do not so.
      DEMETRIUS Stay, on thy peril: I alone will go.   *Exit*
      HELENA O, I am out of breath in this fond chase!
      The more my prayer, the lesser is my grace.
90   Happy is Hermia, wheresoe'er she lies;
      For she hath blessèd and attractive eyes.
      How came her eyes so bright? Not with salt tears:
      If so, my eyes are oftener washed than hers.
      No, no, I am as ugly as a bear;
95   For beasts that meet me run away for fear:

65 **wisher's eyes** i.e. Lysander's   **pressed** i.e. closed in sleep   **68 approve** test   **78 Churl** villain/
scoundrel   **79 owe** own   **80 forbid … eyelid** prevent you from sleeping   **85 charge** command   **haunt**
pursue/hang around   **86 darkling** in the dark   **88 fond** foolish/doting   **89 grace** favour   **90 lies** is/
resides

Therefore no marvel though Demetrius
Do, as a monster, fly my presence thus.
What wicked and dissembling glass of mine
Made me compare with Hermia's sphery eyne?
100   But who is here? Lysander, on the ground;   *Sees Lysander*
Dead, or asleep? I see no blood, no wound.
Lysander if you live, good sir, awake.

LYSANDER And run through fire I will for thy sweet sake.   *Wakes*
Transparent Helena, nature shows her art
105   That through thy bosom makes me see thy heart.
Where is Demetrius? O, how fit a word
Is that vile name to perish on my sword!

HELENA Do not say so, Lysander, say not so.
What though he love your Hermia? Lord, what
    though?
110   Yet Hermia still loves you; then be content.

LYSANDER Content with Hermia? No, I do repent
The tedious minutes I with her have spent.
Not Hermia but Helena now I love;
Who will not change a raven for a dove?
115   The will of man is by his reason swayed,
And reason says you are the worthier maid.
Things growing are not ripe until their season;
So I, being young, till now ripe not to reason.
And touching now the point of human skill,
120   Reason becomes the marshal to my will
And leads me to your eyes, where I o'erlook
Love's stories written in love's richest book.

HELENA Wherefore was I to this keen mockery born?
When at your hands did I deserve this scorn?
125   Is't not enough, is't not enough, young man,
That I did never, no, nor never can,
Deserve a sweet look from Demetrius' eye,
But you must flout my insufficiency?
Good troth you do me wrong, good sooth, you do,
130   In such disdainful manner me to woo.
But fare you well; perforce I must confess
I thought you lord of more true gentleness.

---

96 marvel wonder   **97 as** as if (from)   **98 glass** mirror   **99 sphery eyne** heavenly eyes
104 Transparent radiant/see-through   **art** skill (allowing him to see through Helena's body)   **109 What though** what of it (if)   **115 will** inclination (plays on sense of 'sexual desire'/'penis')   **118 ripe not** i.e. was not mature enough   **119 point** peak   **skill** discernment   **120 marshal** guide   **121 o'erlook** read
122 stories narrative/true history   **123 Wherefore** why   **129 Good troth** truly   **good sooth** indeed
132 lord possessor   **gentleness** nobility/courtesy/kindness

O, that a lady of one man refused
Should of another therefore be abused!   *Exit*

135 **LYSANDER** She sees not Hermia. Hermia, sleep thou there,
And never mayst thou come Lysander near;
For as a surfeit of the sweetest things
The deepest loathing to the stomach brings,
Or as the heresies that men do leave
140 Are hated most of those they did deceive,
So thou, my surfeit and my heresy,
Of all be hated, but the most of me.
And all my powers address your love and might
To honour Helen and to be her knight!   *Exit*

145 **HERMIA** Help me, Lysander, help me; do thy best   *Wakes*
To pluck this crawling serpent from my breast!
Ay me, for pity; what a dream was here?
Lysander, look how I do quake with fear:
Methought a serpent ate my heart away,
150 And you sat smiling at his cruel prey.
Lysander! What, removed? Lysander! Lord!
What, out of hearing? Gone? No sound, no word?
Alack, where are you? Speak, an if you hear:
Speak, of all loves! I swoon almost with fear.
155 No? Then I well perceive you are not nigh.
Either death or you I'll find immediately.   *Titania remains asleep*
                                                        Exit

Act 3 [Scene 1]   *running scene 4 continues*

*Enter the Clowns [Bottom, Quince, Snug, Flute, Snout and
Starveling]*

BOTTOM Are we all met?
QUINCE Pat, pat, and here's a marvellous convenient
place for our rehearsal. This green plot shall be our
stage, this hawthorn brake our tiring-house, and we
5 will do it in action as we will do it before the duke.
BOTTOM Peter Quince?
QUINCE What sayest thou, bully Bottom?
BOTTOM There are things in this comedy of Pyramus and
Thisbe that will never please. First, Pyramus must

134 **of** by   **abused** mistreated   137 **surfeit** excess   139 **leave** renounce   140 **those ... deceive** i.e. the
former heretics themselves   142 **Of** by   143 **address** direct   150 **prey** act of preying   151 **removed**
departed   153 **an if** if   154 **of all loves** for love's sake   3.1 *Clowns* lower-class comic characters   2 **Pat**
punctually   4 **brake** thicket   **tiring-house** dressing-room   7 **bully** old mate, good fellow

10   draw a sword to kill himself; which the ladies cannot
      abide. How answer you that?

      SNOUT By'r lakin, a parlous fear.

      STARVELING I believe we must leave the killing out,
      when all is done.

15   BOTTOM Not a whit: I have a device to make all well.
      Write me a prologue, and let the prologue seem to
      say we will do no harm with our swords, and that
      Pyramus is not killed indeed. And for the more better
      assurance, tell them that I, Pyramus, am not

20   Pyramus, but Bottom the weaver; this will put
      them out of fear.

      QUINCE Well, we will have such a prologue, and it shall
      be written in eight and six.

      BOTTOM No, make it two more: let it be written in eight

25   and eight.

      SNOUT Will not the ladies be afeard of the lion?

      STARVELING I fear it, I promise you.

      BOTTOM Masters, you ought to consider with yourselves,
      to bring in — God shield us! — a lion among ladies is

30   a most dreadful thing. For there is not a more fearful
      wild-fowl than your lion living. And we ought to look
      to it.

      SNOUT Therefore another prologue must tell he is not a
      lion.

35   BOTTOM Nay, you must name his name, and half his face
      must be seen through the lion's neck, and he himself
      must speak through, saying thus, or to the same
      defect: 'Ladies' or 'Fair-ladies, I would wish you' or 'I
      would request you' or 'I would entreat you, not to fear,

40   not to tremble. My life for yours. If you think I come
      hither as a lion, it were pity of my life. No, I am no
      such thing, I am a man as other men are.' And there
      indeed let him name his name, and tell them plainly he
      is Snug the joiner.

45   QUINCE Well, it shall be so. But there is two hard things:
      that is, to bring the moonlight into a chamber, for
      you know Pyramus and Thisbe meet by moonlight.

---

12 By'r lakin by our ladykin (i.e. the Virgin Mary)   **parlous** perilous   **14 done** i.e. said and done
16 Write me write/write for me   **23 eight and six** alternating lines of eight and six syllables (common
metre for ballads)   **26 afeard** afraid   **27 it** either the lion, or that the ladies will be afraid   **30 fearful**
frightening   **31 wild-fowl** i.e. wild beast (literally, bird)   **38 defect** malapropism for 'effect'   **40 My ...
yours** by my life (literally, I would lay down my life for you)   **41 pity ... life** a bad thing, by my life/my life
would be at risk   **43 plainly** may pun on 'plane' (carpenter's tool)

SNOUT Doth the moon shine that night we play our play?

50 BOTTOM A calendar, a calendar! Look in the almanac. Find out moonshine, find out moonshine.   *They consult an almanac*

[*Robin may*] *enter*

QUINCE Yes, it doth shine that night.

BOTTOM Why, then may you leave a casement of the great chamber window, where we play, open, and
55 the moon may shine in at the casement.

QUINCE Ay, or else one must come in with a bush of thorns and a lantern, and say he comes to disfigure, or to present, the person of Moonshine. Then there is another thing: we must have a wall in the great
60 chamber; for Pyramus and Thisbe, says the story, did talk through the chink of a wall.

SNOUT You can never bring in a wall. What say you, Bottom?

BOTTOM Some man or other must present Wall: and let
65 him have some plaster, or some loam, or some rough-cast about him, to signify wall; or let him hold his fingers thus; and through that cranny shall   *Hand gesture*
Pyramus and Thisbe whisper.   *suggesting*

QUINCE If that may be, then all is well. Come, sit down,   *a hole in a wall*
70 every mother's son, and rehearse your parts. Pyramus, you begin: when you have spoken your speech, enter into that brake, and so every one according to his cue.

Robin [*may*] *enter*

ROBIN What hempen home-spuns have we swagg'ring   *Aside*
here,
75 So near the cradle of the fairy queen?
What, a play toward? I'll be an auditor,
An actor too perhaps, if I see cause.

QUINCE Speak, Pyramus.— Thisbe, stand forth.

PYRAMUS [BOTTOM] Thisbe, the flowers of odious savours sweet—

80 QUINCE Odours, odours.

PYRAMUS [BOTTOM] —odours savours sweet,
So hath thy breath, my dearest Thisbe dear.

---

50 almanac calendar   53 casement section of a window   56 bush ... lantern the traditional props of the man in the moon   57 disfigure malapropism for 'figure' (i.e. represent)   58 present represent   66 rough-cast lime and gravel mixture used for plastering walls   70 rehearse recite   74 hempen home-spuns those wearing home-made/rustic clothes   swagg'ring blustering   75 cradle place of rest   76 toward in preparation

But hark, a voice! Stay thou but here awhile,
And by and by I will to thee appear.   *Exit*

85 ROBIN A stranger Pyramus than e'er played here. [*Exit*]
THISBE [FLUTE] Must I speak now?

QUINCE Ay, marry, must you, for you must understand
he goes but to see a noise that he heard, and is to
come again.

90 THISBE [FLUTE] Most radiant Pyramus, most lily-white of
hue,
Of colour like the red rose on triumphant brier,
Most brisky juvenal and eke most lovely Jew,
As true as truest horse that yet would never tire,
I'll meet thee, Pyramus, at Ninny's tomb.

95 QUINCE 'Ninus' tomb', man! Why, you must not speak
that yet; that you answer to Pyramus. You speak all
your part at once, cues and all. Pyramus, enter: your
cue is past; it is, 'never tire'.

THISBE [FLUTE] O — As true as truest horse that yet
would never tire.

Enter [Robin and] Pyramus [Bottom] with the ass head

100 PYRAMUS [BOTTOM] If I were fair, Thisbe, I were only
thine.

QUINCE O monstrous! O strange! We are haunted. Pray,
masters! Fly, masters! Help!   *The Clowns all exit*

ROBIN I'll follow you, I'll lead you about a round,
Through bog, through bush, through brake, through
brier.

105 Sometime a horse I'll be, sometime a hound,
A hog, a headless bear, sometime a fire,
And neigh and bark and grunt and roar and burn,
Like horse, hound, hog, bear, fire, at every
turn.   *Exit* **If Bottom exited**
BOTTOM Why do they run away? This is a knavery of   **with the other**

110 them to make me afeard.   **clowns, he re-enters here**
Enter Snout

SNOUT O Bottom, thou art changed! What do I see on
thee?

BOTTOM What do you see? You see an asshead of your
own, do you?   [*Exit Snout*]

---

84 by and by shortly   **92 brisky juvenal** lively young man   **eke** also   **Jew** desperate rhyme, or perhaps
short for 'juvenal' or 'jewel' as a term of affection   **95 Ninus** founder of the city of Nineveh in what is now
Iraq   **97 part** an actor's written part consisted solely of his lines and cues   **100 fair** handsome   **were**
would be   **103 round** circular dance/circuitous route   **106 fire** will-o'-the-wisp, a flame over marshy
ground (caused by gas but popularly supposed to be a hobgoblin's trick)   **109 knavery** trick

Enter Quince

115 QUINCE Bless thee, Bottom! Bless thee! Thou art
        translated.   *Exit*

BOTTOM I see their knavery: this is to make an ass of me,
        to fright me, if they could; but I will not stir from this
        place, do what they can. I will walk up and down here,
120   and I will sing, that they shall hear I am not afraid.
            The ousel cock so black of hue,   *Sings*
            With orange-tawny bill,
            The throstle with his note so true,
            The wren with little quill—

125 TITANIA What angel wakes me from my flow'ry bed?   *Wakes*
BOTTOM The finch, the sparrow and the lark,   *Sings*
            The plain-song cuckoo grey,
            Whose note full many a man doth mark,
            And dares not answer nay —
130   For, indeed, who would set his wit to so foolish a
        bird? Who would give a bird the lie, though he cry
        'cuckoo' never so?

TITANIA I pray thee, gentle mortal, sing again:
        Mine ear is much enamoured of thy note;
135   So is mine eye enthrallèd to thy shape:
        And thy fair virtue's force perforce doth move me
        On the first view to say, to swear, I love thee.

BOTTOM Methinks, mistress, you should have little
        reason for that: and yet, to say the truth, reason
140   and love keep little company together nowadays; the
        more the pity that some honest neighbours will not
        make them friends. Nay, I can gleek upon occasion.

TITANIA Thou art as wise as thou art beautiful.

BOTTOM Not so, neither: but if I had wit enough to get
145   out of this wood, I have enough to serve mine own
        turn.

TITANIA Out of this wood do not desire to go:
        Thou shalt remain here, whether thou wilt or no.
        I am a spirit of no common rate.
150   The summer still doth tend upon my state,
        And I do love thee: therefore, go with me.
        I'll give thee fairies to attend on thee,

116 **translated** transformed   121 **ousel cock** male blackbird   123 **throstle** song-thrush   124 **quill** reed/
pipe (i.e. voice)   127 **plain-song** melodically simple   129 **dares … nay** is unable to deny the truth of the
cuckoo's cry of 'cuckold' (man with an unfaithful wife)   130 **who … bird** adaptation of 'do not set your wit
against a fool's' (proverbial)   131 **give … lie** accuse the bird of lying   132 **cuckoo** i.e. 'cuckold'   **never
so** ever so much   135 **enthrallèd** enslaved   136 **virtue's** qualities'   **perforce** of necessity   142 **gleek**
make a jest   146 **turn** purposes   148 **wilt** wish to   149 **rate** worth, rank   150 **still** always   **tend upon**
serve, wait upon   **state** status as queen

And they shall fetch thee jewels from the deep,
And sing while thou on pressèd flowers dost sleep.
155 And I will purge thy mortal grossness so
That thou shalt like an airy spirit go.
Peaseblossom, Cobweb, Moth, Mustardseed!
Enter four Fairies
PEASEBLOSSOM Ready.
COBWEB And I.
160 **MOTH** And I.
MUSTARDSEED And I.
ALL Where shall we go?
TITANIA Be kind and courteous to this gentleman.
Hop in his walks and gambol in his eyes,
165 Feed him with apricocks and dewberries,
With purple grapes, green figs, and mulberries.
The honey-bags steal from the humble-bees,
And for night-tapers crop their waxen thighs
And light them at the fiery glow-worm's eyes,
170 To have my love to bed and to arise.
And pluck the wings from painted butterflies
To fan the moonbeams from his sleeping eyes.
Nod to him, elves, and do him courtesies.
PEASEBLOSSOM Hail, mortal!
175 **COBWEB** Hail!
MOTH Hail!
MUSTARDSEED Hail!
BOTTOM I cry your worship's mercy, heartily; I beseech   *To Cobweb*
your worship's name.
180 **COBWEB** Cobweb.
BOTTOM I shall desire you of more acquaintance, good
Master Cobweb: if I cut my finger, I shall make bold
with you.— Your name, honest gentleman?
PEASEBLOSSOM Peaseblossom.
185 **BOTTOM** I pray you commend me to Mistress Squash,
your mother, and to Master Peascod, your father.
Good Master Peaseblossom, I shall desire you of more
acquaintance too.— Your name, I beseech you, sir?
MUSTARDSEED Mustardseed.

---

153 deep bottom of the sea   **155 grossness** bodily form   **157 Peaseblossom** flower of plants of the pea family; **Pease** also meant 'something of very small value or importance'   **Moth** pronounced 'mote' (i.e. speck) so this sense may also be implied   **164 eyes** i.e. sight   **165 apricocks** apricots   **dewberries** type of blackberry   **167 humble-bees** bumble-bees   **168 night-tapers** candles   **170 arise** possible erectile connotations   **178 cry … mercy** beg your pardon   **181 desire … acquaintance** want to be better acquainted with you   **182 if … you** cobwebs were used to stop bleeding   **185 Squash** unripe pea-pod   **186 Peascod** pea-pod (a traditional remedy for lovesickness, with play on 'codpiece')

190 **BOTTOM** Good Master Mustardseed, I know your
      patience well: that same cowardly, giant-like ox-
      beef hath devoured many a gentleman of your house.
      I promise you, your kindred hath made my eyes
      water ere now. I desire you of more acquaintance,
195   good Master Mustardseed.
   TITANIA Come, wait upon him, lead him to my bower.
      The moon methinks looks with a wat'ry eye,
      And when she weeps, weeps every little flower,
      Lamenting some enforcèd chastity.
200 Tie up my lover's tongue, bring him silently. *Exeunt*

[Act 3 Scene 2]   *running scene 5*

Enter King of Fairies [Oberon] alone

   OBERON I wonder if Titania be awaked;
      Then what it was that next came in her eye,
      Which she must dote on in extremity.
   Enter [Robin] Puck
      Here comes my messenger.— How now, mad spirit?
5   What night-rule now about this haunted grove?
   ROBIN My mistress with a monster is in love.
      Near to her close and consecrated bower,
      While she was in her dull and sleeping hour,
      A crew of patches, rude mechanicals,
10   That work for bread upon Athenian stalls,
      Were met together to rehearse a play
      Intended for great Theseus' nuptial-day.
      The shallowest thick-skin of that barren sort,
      Who Pyramus presented in their sport,
15   Forsook his scene and entered in a brake,
      When I did him at this advantage take:
      An ass's noll I fixèd on his head.
      Anon his Thisbe must be answerèd,
      And forth my mimic comes. When they him spy,
20   As wild geese that the creeping fowler eye,
      Or russet-pated choughs, many in sort,

191 **patience** endurance (as mustard is eaten with beef)   193 **made ... water** since mustard is hot in the mouth   198 **weeps** i.e. causes dew   199 **enforcèd** violated   200 **Tie ... tongue** perhaps because Bottom is braying   3.2   3 **in extremity** to excess   5 **night-rule** mischievous, disordered night-time activity **haunted** much frequented   7 **close** private/secluded   8 **dull** inactive   9 **patches** clowns/fools   **rude mechanicals** uneducated manual workers   13 **barren sort** stupid group   15 **Forsook** left   **scene** performance space   17 **noll** head   19 **mimic** burlesque actor/performer   20 **fowler** hunter   21 **russet-pated choughs** reddish-brown jackdaws (with play on 'chuff', rustic boor)   **many in sort** i.e. in a large flock

Rising and cawing at the gun's report,
Sever themselves and madly sweep the sky,
So, at his sight, away his fellows fly.

25 And at our stamp here o'er and o'er one falls;
He 'murder' cries and help from Athens calls.
Their sense thus weak, lost with their fears thus strong,
Made senseless things begin to do them wrong.
For briars and thorns at their apparel snatch,

30 Some sleeves, some hats, from yielders all things catch.
I led them on in this distracted fear,
And left sweet Pyramus translated there:
When in that moment, so it came to pass,
Titania waked and straightway loved an ass.

35 **OBERON** This falls out better than I could devise.
But hast thou yet latched the Athenian's eyes
With the love juice, as I did bid thee do?
ROBIN I took him sleeping — that is finished too —
And the Athenian woman by his side,

40 That, when he waked, of force she must be eyed.
Enter Demetrius and Hermia
OBERON Stand close. This is the same Athenian.   *They stand aside*
ROBIN This is the woman, but not this the man.
DEMETRIUS O, why rebuke you him that loves you so?
Lay breath so bitter on your bitter foe.

45 **HERMIA** Now I but chide, but I should use thee worse,
For thou, I fear, hast given me cause to curse,
If thou hast slain Lysander in his sleep,
Being o'er shoes in blood, plunge in the deep,
And kill me too.

50 The sun was not so true unto the day
As he to me. Would he have stol'n away
From sleeping Hermia? I'll believe as soon
This whole earth may be bored and that the moon
May through the centre creep, and so displease

55 Her brother's noontide with th'Antipodes.
It cannot be but thou hast murdered him,
So should a murderer look, so dead, so grim.
DEMETRIUS So should the murdered look, and so should I,
Pierced through the heart with your stern cruelty:

---

22 **report** sound of firing   23 **Sever** scatter   **sweep** move swiftly across   30 **yielders** those who give
something up/those who yield to fear   36 **latched** ensnared/wetted   40 **of force** by necessity   41 **close**
concealed   45 **chide** rebuke (you)   **use** treat   48 **Being o'er shoes** having waded   50 **true** loyal
53 **whole** solid, intact   **bored** pierced through   54 **centre** i.e. of the earth   55 **Her brother's** i.e. the sun's
th'Antipodes the people/places on the opposite side of the globe   57 **dead** deadly/murderous

60   Yet you, the murderer, looks as bright, as clear,
          As yonder Venus in her glimm'ring sphere.
     HERMIA What's this to my Lysander? Where is he?
          Ah, good Demetrius, wilt thou give him me?
     DEMETRIUS I'd rather give his carcass to my hounds.
65   HERMIA Out, dog! Out, cur! Thou driv'st me past the bounds
          Of maiden's patience. Hast thou slain him, then?
          Henceforth be never numbered among men.
          O, once tell true, tell true even for my sake!
          Durst thou a looked upon him being awake?
70   And hast thou killed him sleeping? O brave touch!
          Could not a worm, an adder, do so much?
          An adder did it, for with doubler tongue
          Than thine, thou serpent, never adder stung.
     DEMETRIUS You spend your passion on a misprised mood.
75   I am not guilty of Lysander's blood,
          Nor is he dead, for aught that I can tell.
     HERMIA I pray thee tell me then that he is well.
     DEMETRIUS An if I could, what should I get therefor?
     HERMIA A privilege never to see me more;
80   And from thy hated presence part I so:
          See me no more, whether he be dead or no.   *Exit*
     DEMETRIUS There is no following her in this fierce vein:
          Here therefore for a while I will remain.
          So sorrow's heaviness doth heavier grow
85   For debt that bankrupt sleep doth sorrow owe,
          Which now in some slight measure it will pay,
          If for his tender here I make some stay.
                         [*Demetrius*] *lies down* [*and sleeps*]
     OBERON What hast thou done? Thou hast mistaken quite
          And laid the love juice on some true love's sight:
90   Of thy misprision must perforce ensue
          Some true love turned, and not a false turned true.
     ROBIN Then fate o'errules, that, one man holding troth,
          A million fail, confounding oath on oath.
     OBERON About the wood go swifter than the wind,
95   And Helena of Athens look thou find.

61 Venus bright planet; also Roman goddess of love   sphere orbit/hollow surrounding sphere   62 to got
to do with   65 cur dog   67 numbered counted   68 once once and for all   69 Durst would you/did you
dare   a have   70 brave touch fine/impudent deed   71 worm snake   72 doubler more divided/
deceitful   74 spend expend/waste   passion powerful feelings   misprised mood mistaken anger
78 therefor for it   82 vein mood   84 So ... owe i.e. lack of sleep and sorrow combined are making me
very tired   heavier harder to bear/sleepier   85 For because of the   87 his tender sleep's offer   make
some stay stay here awhile   88 quite utterly   90 misprision error   92 one ... troth for each man who
keeps his word/faith in love   93 confounding breaking   on after   95 look be sure

All fancy-sick she is and pale of cheer,
With sighs of love, that costs the fresh blood dear.
By some illusion see thou bring her here.
I'll charm his eyes against she doth appear.
100 **ROBIN** I go, I go, look how I go,
Swifter than arrow from the Tartar's bow.   *Exit*
OBERON Flower of this purple dye,   *Squeezes juice*
Hit with Cupid's archery,   *on Demetrius'*
Sink in apple of his eye.   *eyes*
105 When his love he doth espy,
Let her shine as glor'ously
As the Venus of the sky.
When thou wak'st, if she be by,
Beg of her for remedy.
Enter [Robin] Puck
110 **ROBIN** Captain of our fairy band,
Helena is here at hand,
And the youth, mistook by me,
Pleading for a lover's fee.
Shall we their fond pageant see?
115 Lord, what fools these mortals be!
OBERON Stand aside: the noise they make
Will cause Demetrius to awake.   *They stand aside*
ROBIN Then will two at once woo one,
That must needs be sport alone.
120 And those things do best please me
That befall preposterously.
Enter Lysander [following] Helena
LYSANDER Why should you think that I should woo in
scorn?
Scorn and derision never come in tears:
Look when I vow, I weep; and vows so born,
125 In their nativity all truth appears.
How can these things in me seem scorn to you,
Bearing the badge of faith to prove them true?
HELENA You do advance your cunning more and more.
When truth kills truth, O devilish-holy fray!

96 **fancy-sick** lovesick   **cheer** face   97 **sighs** … **dear** each sigh was thought to drain a drop of blood from the heart   98 **illusion** deception   99 **against** in preparation for when   101 **Tartar's bow** powerful bow from Central Asia   104 **apple** pupil/centre   109 **remedy** relief, resolution   113 **fee** payment   114 **fond pageant** foolish spectacle   119 **alone** unique/on its own   121 **preposterously** perversely, out of the normal course of events   124 **Look when** whenever   125 **nativity** i.e. through weeping   127 **badge** outward sign (as worn on servants' livery), i.e. tears   128 **advance** show   129 **truth kills truth** i.e. his vows to Hermia and to Helena invalidate one another   **devilish-holy fray** quarrel involving false and true vows

130   These vows are Hermia's. Will you give her o'er?
       Weigh oath with oath, and you will nothing weigh.
       Your vows to her and me, put in two scales,
       Will even weigh, and both as light as tales.
       LYSANDER I had no judgement when to her I swore.
135   **HELENA** Nor none, in my mind, now you give her o'er.
       LYSANDER Demetrius loves her, and he you.
       DEMETRIUS O Helen, goddess, nymph, perfect, divine!

                                                    Awakes

       To what, my love, shall I compare thine eyne?
       Crystal is muddy. O, how ripe in show
140   Thy lips, those kissing cherries, tempting grow!
       That pure congealèd white, high Taurus' snow,
       Fanned with the eastern wind, turns to a crow
       When thou hold'st up thy hand. O, let me kiss
       This princess of pure white, this seal of bliss!
145   **HELENA** O spite! O hell! I see you all are bent
       To set against me for your merriment:
       If you were civil and knew courtesy,
       You would not do me thus much injury.
       Can you not hate me, as I know you do,
150   But you must join in souls to mock me too?
       If you were men, as men you are in show,
       You would not use a gentle lady so;
       To vow, and swear, and superpraise my parts,
       When I am sure you hate me with your hearts.
155   You both are rivals and love Hermia;
       And now both rivals to mock Helena.
       A trim exploit, a manly enterprise,
       To conjure tears up in a poor maid's eyes
       With your derision; none of noble sort
160   Would so offend a virgin and extort
       A poor soul's patience, all to make you sport.
       LYSANDER You are unkind, Demetrius; be not so,
       For you love Hermia; this you know I know;
       And here, with all good will, with all my heart,
165   In Hermia's love I yield you up my part;

130 **o'er** up   133 **light as tales** false as rumours/lies   136 **Demetrius . . . you** there may be a missing rhyme line for Helena hereafter   139 **ripe** i.e. full and red   **show** appearance   141 **pure congealèd white** i.e. pale skin (considered to be especially beautiful)   **Taurus** mountain range in Turkey   142 **turns . . . crow** seems black in comparison (with Helena's white skin)   144 **seal** promise   145 **bent** disposed   146 **set against** be hostile to   148 **do . . . injury** insult me so much   150 **join in souls** unite   152 **gentle** noble/mild   153 **superpraise** praise excessively   **parts** qualities   157 **trim** fine   160 **extort** torture/wring

And yours of Helena to me bequeath,
Whom I do love and will do till my death.

HELENA Never did mockers waste more idle breath.

DEMETRIUS Lysander, keep thy Hermia, I will none:

170 If e'er I loved her, all that love is gone.
My heart to her but as guestwise sojourned,
And now to Helen is it home returned,
There to remain.

LYSANDER Helen, it is not so.

175 **DEMETRIUS** Disparage not the faith thou dost not know,
Lest to thy peril thou abide it dear.
Look where thy love comes, yonder is thy dear.

Enter Hermia

HERMIA Dark night, that from the eye his function takes,
The ear more quick of apprehension makes,

180 Wherein it doth impair the seeing sense,
It pays the hearing double recompense.
Thou art not by mine eye, Lysander, found,
Mine ear, I thank it, brought me to thy sound.
But why unkindly didst thou leave me so?

185 **LYSANDER** Why should he stay whom love doth press
to go?

HERMIA What love could press Lysander from my side?

LYSANDER Lysander's love, that would not let him bide —
Fair Helena, who more engilds the night
Than all yon fiery oes and eyes of light.—

190 Why seek'st thou me? Could not this make thee   *To Hermia*
know,
The hate I bear thee made me leave thee so?

HERMIA You speak not as you think; it cannot be.

HELENA Lo, she is one of this confed'racy!
Now I perceive they have conjoined all three

195 To fashion this false sport in spite of me.
Injurious Hermia, most ungrateful maid,
Have you conspired, have you with these contrived
To bait me with this foul derision?
Is all the counsel that we two have shared,

200 The sisters' vows, the hours that we have spent,
When we have chid the hasty-footed time

---

169 **will none** i.e. want nothing to do with her   171 **but … sojourned** stayed with her merely as a visitor
176 **abide** suffer for/pay for   **dear** at great cost   178 **his** its   179 **apprehension** perception   186 **press**
urge   187 **bide** remain   188 **engilds** brightens with gold   189 **yon** i.e. those over there   **oes** spangles
(i.e. stars)   193 **confed'racy** alliance   195 **fashion** contrive   **in spite** to vex   196 **Injurious** harmful,
unjust   198 **bait** persecute/torment   199 **counsel** inmost thoughts/advice   201 **chid** scolded

For parting us — O, is all forgot?
All schooldays' friendship, childhood innocence?
We, Hermia, like two artificial gods,
205   Have with our needles created both one flower,
Both on one sampler, sitting on one cushion,
Both warbling of one song, both in one key,
As if our hands, our sides, voices and minds,
Had been incorporate. So we grew together
210   Like to a double cherry, seeming parted,
But yet a union in partition,
Two lovely berries moulded on one stem,
So with two seeming bodies but one heart,
Two of the first, like coats in heraldry,
215   Due but to one and crownèd with one crest.
And will you rent our ancient love asunder,
To join with men in scorning your poor friend?
It is not friendly, 'tis not maidenly.
Our sex, as well as I, may chide you for it,
220   Though I alone do feel the injury.
HERMIA I am amazèd at your passionate words.
I scorn you not; it seems that you scorn me.
HELENA Have you not set Lysander, as in scorn,
To follow me and praise my eyes and face?
225   And made your other love, Demetrius,
Who even but now did spurn me with his foot,
To call me goddess, nymph, divine and rare,
Precious, celestial? Wherefore speaks he this
To her he hates? And wherefore doth Lysander
230   Deny your love, so rich within his soul,
And tender me, forsooth, affection,
But by your setting on, by your consent?
What though I be not so in grace as you,
So hung upon with love, so fortunate,
235   But miserable most, to love unloved?
This you should pity rather than despise.
HERMIA I understand not what you mean by this.
HELENA Ay, do. Persever, counterfeit sad looks,
Make mouths upon me when I turn my back,

---

204 artificial skilled in the arts of creation   **207 one key** total harmony   **209 incorporate** indivisible, one body   **210 Like** similar   **213 heart** may pun on 'hart', a common heraldic device   **214 first** i.e. **bodies** (plays on sense of 'dominant colour on a shield')   **coats** coats of arms (which can appear twice on a shield though under **one crest**)   **215 Due … one** a coat of arms is allocated to a specific individual   **216 rent** rend, tear   **ancient** long-standing   **asunder** apart   **227 rare** splendid/exceptional   **231 tender** offer   **233 grace** favour   **238 Persever** persevere   **sad** solemn   **239 mouths** faces

240　　　Wink each at other, hold the sweet jest up:
　　　　This sport well carried shall be chronicled.
　　　　If you have any pity, grace, or manners,
　　　　You would not make me such an argument.
　　　　But fare ye well. 'Tis partly my own fault,
245　　　Which death or absence soon shall remedy.
　LYSANDER Stay, gentle Helena, hear my excuse:
　　　　My love, my life, my soul, fair Helena!
　HELENA O excellent!
　HERMIA Sweet, do not scorn her so.　　　　　　　*To Lysander*
250　DEMETRIUS If she cannot entreat, I can compel.　　*To Lysander*
　LYSANDER Thou canst compel no more than she entreat.
　　　　Thy threats have no more strength than her weak
　　　　　prayers.
　　　　Helen, I love thee, by my life, I do;
　　　　I swear by that which I will lose for thee,
255　　　To prove him false that says I love thee not.
　DEMETRIUS I say I love thee more than he can do.　　*To Helena*
　LYSANDER If thou say so, withdraw, and prove it too.
　DEMETRIUS Quick, come!
　HERMIA Lysander, whereto tends all this?　　*She hangs on Lysander*
260　LYSANDER Away, you Ethiope!
　DEMETRIUS No, no, sir,
　　　　Seem to break loose; take on as you would follow,
　　　　But yet come not: you are a tame man, go!
　LYSANDER Hang off, thou cat, thou burr! Vile thing, let
　　　　　loose,
265　　　Or I will shake thee from me like a serpent!
　HERMIA Why are you grown so rude?
　　　　What change is this, sweet love?
　LYSANDER Thy love? Out, tawny Tartar, out!
　　　　Out, loathèd medicine! O hated potion, hence!
270　HERMIA Do you not jest?
　HELENA Yes, sooth, and so do you.
　LYSANDER Demetrius, I will keep my word with thee.
　DEMETRIUS I would I had your bond, for I perceive
　　　　A weak bond holds you; I'll not trust your word.

---

240 **hold ... up** maintain the joke   241 **carried** conducted   243 **argument** subject (for a joke)
257 **withdraw** i.e. remove yourself from present company (for a duel)   259 **whereto** to what end
260 **Ethiope** Ethiopian, i.e. dark-complexioned (in contrast to fair Helena)   262 **take on as** behave as if
264 **Hang off** leave hold   **burr** prickly seed-head that sticks easily to clothing   **let loose** get off
266 **rude** harsh, unkind, offensive   268 **Out** exclamation of impatience ('get away!')   **tawny** dark-skinned
Tartar person from central Asia   269 **medicine** i.e. poison   271 **sooth** truly   274 **weak bond** i.e. Hermia
(plays on earlier sense of 'oath')

275   **LYSANDER** What, should I hurt her, strike her, kill her
      dead?
      Although I hate her, I'll not harm her so.
      HERMIA What, can you do me greater harm than hate?
      Hate me? Wherefore? O me! What news, my love?
      Am not I Hermia? Are not you Lysander?
280   I am as fair now as I was erewhile.
      Since night you loved me; yet since night you left me.
      Why, then you left me — O, the gods forbid! —
      In earnest, shall I say?
      LYSANDER Ay, by my life;
285   And never did desire to see thee more.
      Therefore be out of hope, of question, of doubt;
      Be certain, nothing truer: 'tis no jest
      That I do hate thee and love Helena.
      HERMIA O me! You juggler, you canker-blossom,   *To Helena*
290   You thief of love! What, have you come by night
      And stolen my love's heart from him?
      HELENA Fine, i'faith!
      Have you no modesty, no maiden shame,
      No touch of bashfulness? What, will you tear
295   Impatient answers from my gentle tongue?
      Fie, fie! You counterfeit, you puppet, you!
      HERMIA Puppet? Why so? Ay, that way goes the game.
      Now I perceive that she hath made compare
      Between our statures, she hath urged her height,
300   And with her personage, her tall personage,
      Her height, forsooth, she hath prevailed with him.
      And are you grown so high in his esteem
      Because I am so dwarfish and so low?
      How low am I, thou painted maypole? Speak!
305   How low am I? I am not yet so low
      But that my nails can reach unto thine eyes.   *Attacks her*
      HELENA I pray you, though you mock me, gentlemen,
      Let her not hurt me; I was never curst,
      I have no gift at all in shrewishness;
310   I am a right maid for my cowardice;
      Let her not strike me. You perhaps may think,

---

280 **erewhile** before   286 **out of** free from   289 **juggler** trickster   **canker-blossom** flower-destroying
worm   295 **Impatient** angry   296 **puppet** false,thing/small person   299 **urged** insisted on/brought
forward   300 **personage** appearance   304 **painted** made-up (with cosmetics)   **maypole** i.e. tall, skinny
person   308 **curst** ill-tempered   309 **shrewishness** scolding/bad temper   310 **right** true/typical

Because she is something lower than myself,
That I can match her.

HERMIA Lower? Hark, again.

315 **HELENA** Good Hermia, do not be so bitter with me.
I evermore did love you, Hermia,
Did ever keep your counsels, never wronged you,
Save that, in love unto Demetrius,
I told him of your stealth unto this wood.

320 He followed you. For love I followed him.
But he hath chid me hence and threatened me
To strike me, spurn me, nay, to kill me too;
And now, so you will let me quiet go,
To Athens will I bear my folly back

325 And follow you no further. Let me go.
You see how simple and how fond I am.

HERMIA Why, get you gone: who is't that hinders you?

HELENA A foolish heart, that I leave here behind.

HERMIA What, with Lysander?

330 **HELENA** With Demetrius.

LYSANDER Be not afraid: she shall not harm thee, Helena.

DEMETRIUS No, sir, she shall not, though you take her part.

HELENA O, when she's angry, she is keen and shrewd.
She was a vixen when she went to school,

335 And though she be but little, she is fierce.

HERMIA 'Little' again! Nothing but 'low' and 'little'?
Why will you suffer her to flout me thus?
Let me come to her.

LYSANDER Get you gone, you dwarf,

340 You minimus, of hind'ring knot-grass made!
You bead, you acorn.

DEMETRIUS You are too officious
In her behalf that scorns your services.
Let her alone. Speak not of Helena,

345 Take not her part. For if thou dost intend
Never so little show of love to her,
Thou shalt abide it.

LYSANDER Now she holds me not.
Now follow, if thou dar'st, to try whose right,

350 Of thine or mine, is most in Helena.

---

312 something lower somewhat shorter   **316 evermore** always   **319 stealth** stealing away   **321 chid me hence** tried to drive me away with scolding   **323 so** if   **326 fond** foolish   **332 part** side   **333 keen** sharp   **shrewd** vicious   **337 suffer** allow   **340 minimus** tiny, insignificant being   **knot-grass** type of creeping weed   **347 abide** pay for

DEMETRIUS Follow? Nay, I'll go with thee, cheek by jowl.

Exeunt Lysander and Demetrius

HERMIA You, mistress, all this coil is 'long of you.

Nay, go not back.

HELENA I will not trust you, I,

355   Nor longer stay in your curst company.

Your hands than mine are quicker for a fray,

My legs are longer though, to run away.

[*Exit Helena, running, followed by Hermia*]

Enter Oberon and [Robin] Puck [coming forward]

OBERON This is thy negligence. Still thou mistak'st,

Or else committ'st thy knaveries wilfully.

360   **ROBIN** Believe me, king of shadows, I mistook.

Did not you tell me I should know the man

By the Athenian garments he hath on?

And so far blameless proves my enterprise,

That I have 'nointed an Athenian's eyes,

365   And so far am I glad it so did sort,

As this their jangling I esteem a sport.

OBERON Thou see'st these lovers seek a place to fight:

Hie therefore, Robin, overcast the night,

The starry welkin cover thou anon

370   With drooping fog as black as Acheron,

And lead these testy rivals so astray

As one come not within another's way.

Like to Lysander sometime frame thy tongue,

Then stir Demetrius up with bitter wrong;

375   And sometime rail thou like Demetrius;

And from each other look thou lead them thus,

Till o'er their brows death-counterfeiting sleep

With leaden legs and batty wings doth creep;

Then crush this herb into Lysander's eye,   *Gives herb*

380   Whose liquor hath this virtuous property,

To take from thence all error with his might,

And make his eyeballs roll with wonted sight.

When they next wake, all this derision

Shall seem a dream and fruitless vision,

---

351 **cheek by jowl** i.e. side by side   352 **coil** turmoil   **'long** on account   *Exit ... Hermia* the Quarto text gives Hermia the exit line 'I am amazed and know not what to say'; Folio's omission of this was probably a printer's error, but it might conceivably have been the purposeful cut of a weak line that converts a rhyming couplet to a triplet   365 **sort** fall out   366 **As** in that   **jangling** squabbling   368 **Hie** hasten   369 **welkin** sky   370 **drooping** falling   **Acheron** one of the four rivers of Hades (the classical underworld)   371 **testy** irritable   372 **As** so that   373 **Like ... tongue** sometimes imitate Lysander's voice   374 **wrong** insults   375 **rail** rant   378 **batty** bat-like   379 **herb** i.e. the antidote   380 **liquor** liquid, juice   **virtuous** powerful   381 **his** its   382 **wonted** accustomed, former   383 **derision** ridiculousness

385　And back to Athens shall the lovers wend
　　　With league whose date till death shall never end.
　　　Whiles I in this affair do thee employ,
　　　I'll to my queen and beg her Indian boy;
　　　And then I will her charmèd eye release
390　From monster's view, and all things shall be peace.
ROBIN My fairy lord, this must be done with haste,
　　　For night-swift dragons cut the clouds full fast,
　　　And yonder shines Aurora's harbinger,
　　　At whose approach, ghosts, wand'ring here and there,
395　Troop home to churchyards; damnèd spirits all,
　　　That in crossways and floods have burial,
　　　Already to their wormy beds are gone;
　　　For fear lest day should look their shames upon,
　　　They wilfully themselves exile from light
400　And must for aye consort with black-browed night.
OBERON But we are spirits of another sort:
　　　I with the morning's love have oft made sport,
　　　And, like a forester, the groves may tread,
　　　Even till the eastern gate, all fiery red,
405　Opening on Neptune with fair blessèd beams,
　　　Turns into yellow gold his salt green streams.
　　　But notwithstanding, haste, make no delay:
　　　We may effect this business yet ere day.　　　　*Exit*
ROBIN Up and down, up and down,
410　　　I will lead them up and down.
　　　　I am feared in field and town.
　　　　Goblin, lead them up and down.
　　　Here comes one.
Enter Lysander
LYSANDER Where art thou, proud Demetrius? Speak
　　　thou now.
415 ROBIN Here, villain, drawn and ready. Where art thou?　　*Imitating*
LYSANDER I will be with thee straight.　　　　　　　　　　　*Demetrius*
ROBIN Follow me, then, to plainer ground.　　　　　　　*Exit Lysander,*
Enter Demetrius　　　　　　　　　　　　　　　　　*following the voice*

---

385 wend make their way　**386 league** alliance, friendship　**date** duration　**392 dragons** supposedly pulling the chariot of night or the moon　**cut** cut through　**393 Aurora's harbinger** the morning star, which can be seen before dawn　**396 crossways** crossroads, the unconsecrated burial place for suicides　**floods** 'burial' place of those who had drowned (and whose bodies were unrecoverable)　**400 aye** eternity　**consort** keep company　**402 morning's love** either Aurora's lover, or Aurora, Roman goddess of the dawn (i.e. Oberon does not have to disappear before dawn like the other spirits)　**made sport** amused myself/ made love to　**403 forester** guardian of the forest　**405 Neptune** Roman god of the sea　**412 Goblin** Puck refers to himself　**415 drawn** with sword drawn　**416 straight** at once　**417 plainer** flatter/more open

DEMETRIUS Lysander, speak again;
    Thou runaway, thou coward, art thou fled?
420   Speak! In some bush? Where dost thou hide thy head?
ROBIN Thou coward, art thou bragging to the stars,   *Imitating Lysander*
    Telling the bushes that thou look'st for wars,
    And wilt not come? Come, recreant, come, thou child.
    I'll whip thee with a rod. He is defiled
425   That draws a sword on thee.
DEMETRIUS Yea, art thou there?
ROBIN Follow my voice. We'll try no manhood here.

                                         Exeunt

Enter Lysander
LYSANDER He goes before me and still dares me on.
    When I come where he calls, then he's gone.
430   The villain is much lighter-heeled than I:
    I followed fast, but faster he did fly;
    That fallen am I in dark uneven way,
    And here will rest me. Come, thou gentle day!

                                         Lie down

    For if but once thou show me thy grey light,
435   I'll find Demetrius and revenge this spite.   *He sleeps*
Enter Robin and Demetrius, shifting places
ROBIN Ho, ho, ho! Coward, why com'st thou not?
DEMETRIUS Abide me, if thou dar'st, for well I wot
    Thou runn'st before me, shifting every place,
    And dar'st not stand, nor look me in the face.
440   Where art thou now?
ROBIN Come hither. I am here.
DEMETRIUS Nay then, thou mock'st me. Thou shalt buy
    this dear
    If ever I thy face by daylight see.
    Now, go thy way: faintness constraineth me
445   To measure out my length on this cold bed.
    By day's approach look to be visited.   *Lies down and sleeps*
Enter Helena
HELENA O weary night, O long and tedious night,
    Abate thy hours! Shine comforts from the east,
    That I may back to Athens by daylight,
450   From these that my poor company detest;
    And sleep, that sometime shuts up sorrow's eye,
    Steal me awhile from mine own company.   *Sleep*

---

423 recreant coward   **427 try** test   **435 spite** vexation, grievance   **437 Abide** confront/endure   **wot**
know   **442 buy** pay for   **444 constraineth** compels   **448 Abate** shorten

ROBIN Yet but three? Come one more,
　　Two of both kinds make up four.
455　Here she comes, curst and sad.
　　Cupid is a knavish lad,
Enter Hermia
　　Thus to make poor females mad.
HERMIA Never so weary, never so in woe,
　　Bedabbled with the dew and torn with briers,
460　I can no further crawl, no further go;
　　My legs can keep no pace with my desires.
　　Here will I rest me till the break of day.
　　Heavens shield Lysander, if they mean a fray!　*Lies down and sleeps*
ROBIN On the ground
465　Sleep sound.
　　I'll apply
　　To your eye,
　　Gentle lover, remedy.　　　　　　*Squeezes the juice*
　　When thou wak'st,　　　　　　*on Lysander's eyes*
470　Thou tak'st
　　True delight
　　In the sight
　　Of thy former lady's eye,
　　And the country proverb known,
475　That every man should take his own,
　　In your waking shall be shown.
　　Jack shall have Jill,
　　Naught shall go ill,
　　The man shall have his mare again, and all shall
　　　　be well.　　　　　　　　　*Exit*
　　　　　　　　They [Lysander, Demetrius,
　　　　　　Helena and Hermia] sleep all the act

Act 4 [Scene 1]　　　　　　*running scene 5 continues*

*Enter Queen of Fairies [Titania] and Clown [Bottom, with ass
head, wearing a coronet of flowers] and Fairies
[Peaseblossom, Cobweb, Moth, Mustardseed] and the King
[Oberon] behind them*

TITANIA Come, sit thee down upon this flow'ry bed,
　　While I thy amiable cheeks do coy,

477 Jack ... Jill 'all shall be well and Jack shall have Jill' (proverbial)　**478 Naught** nothing　**479 man ...
mare** proverbial　**4.1　2 amiable** lovable　**coy** caress

And stick musk-roses in thy sleek smooth head,
And kiss thy fair large ears, my gentle joy.   ⌊*She fondles him*⌋

5 **BOTTOM** Where's Peaseblossom?

PEASEBLOSSOM Ready.

BOTTOM Scratch my head, Peaseblossom. Where's
Monsieur Cobweb?

COBWEB Ready.

10 **BOTTOM** Monsieur Cobweb, good monsieur, get you your
weapons in your hand, and kill me a red-hipped
humble-bee on the top of a thistle; and, good
monsieur, bring me the honey-bag. Do not fret
yourself too much in the action, monsieur; and, good
15 monsieur, have a care the honey-bag break not. I
would be loath to have you overflown with a honey-
bag, signior. Where's Monsieur Mustardseed?   *Cobweb may exit*

MUSTARDSEED Ready.

BOTTOM Give me your neaf, Monsieur Mustardseed.
20 Pray you leave your courtesy, good monsieur.

MUSTARDSEED What's your will?

BOTTOM Nothing, good monsieur, but to help Cavalery
Cobweb to scratch. I must to the barber's, monsieur,
for methinks I am marvellous hairy about the face.
25 And I am such a tender ass, if my hair do but tickle
me, I must scratch.

TITANIA What, wilt thou hear some music, my sweet love?

BOTTOM I have a reasonable good ear in music. Let us
have the tongs and the bones.

Music: tongs, rural music

30 **TITANIA** Or say, sweet love, what thou desirest to eat.

BOTTOM Truly, a peck of provender; I could munch your
good dry oats. Methinks I have a great desire to a
bottle of hay: good hay, sweet hay, hath no fellow.

TITANIA I have a vent'rous fairy that shall seek
35 The squirrel's hoard, and fetch thee new nuts.

BOTTOM I had rather have a handful or two of dried
peas. But, I pray you let none of your people stir me. I
have an exposition of sleep come upon me.

---

16 **overflown** flowed over, drenched   19 **neaf** fist   20 **leave your courtesy** stop bowing/put your hat
back on   22 **Cavalery** cavalier (i.e. courtly gentleman)   23 **Cobweb** apparently an error for
Peaseblossom   24 **marvellous** extremely   29 **tongs** simple metal musical instrument, struck to produce
sound   **bones** pieces of bone clapped together between the fingers   *rural music* simple rustic music
31 **peck** quantity (quarter of a bushel)   **provender** fodder (for animals)   33 **bottle** bundle   **fellow** equal
34 **vent'rous** adventurous, daring   37 **stir** wake   38 **exposition of** malapropism for 'disposition to'

TITANIA Sleep thou, and I will wind thee in my arms.
40   Fairies, begone, and be all ways away. [*Exeunt fairies*]
        So doth the woodbine the sweet honeysuckle
        Gently entwist; the female ivy so
        Enrings the barky fingers of the elm.
        O, how I love thee! How I dote on thee!   *They sleep*
        Enter Robin Goodfellow and Oberon [who comes forward]
45   OBERON Welcome, good Robin.
        See'st thou this sweet sight?
        Her dotage now I do begin to pity.
        For, meeting her of late behind the wood,
        Seeking sweet favours for this hateful fool,
50   I did upbraid her and fall out with her.
        For she his hairy temples then had rounded
        With coronet of fresh and fragrant flowers.
        And that same dew, which sometime on the buds
        Was wont to swell like round and orient pearls,
55   Stood now within the pretty flowerets' eyes
        Like tears that did their own disgrace bewail.
        When I had at my pleasure taunted her,
        And she in mild terms begged my patience,
        I then did ask of her her changeling child,
60   Which straight she gave me, and her fairy sent
        To bear him to my bower in fairy land.
        And now I have the boy, I will undo
        This hateful imperfection of her eyes.
        And, gentle Puck, take this transformèd scalp
65   From off the head of this Athenian swain;
        That, he awaking when the other do,
        May all to Athens back again repair,
        And think no more of this night's accidents
        But as the fierce vexation of a dream.
70   But first I will release the fairy queen.
        Be thou as thou wast wont to be;   *Squeezes the herb on her eyes*
        See as thou wast wont to see.
        Dian's bud o'er Cupid's flower
        Hath such force and blessèd power.
75   Now, my Titania, wake you, my sweet queen.

---

40 **all ways away** gone in all directions   41 **woodbine** bindweed, which entwines itself with
honeysuckle   43 **Enrings** encircles   47 **dotage** infatuation   49 **favours** love tokens (perhaps flowers)
53 **sometime** formerly   54 **orient** from the east/lustrous   55 **flowerets** small flowers   65 **swain** rustic
66 **other** others   67 **repair** make their way   68 **accidents** events   73 **Dian's bud** i.e. Oberon's corrective
herb, linked to Diana, Roman goddess of chastity

TITANIA My Oberon! What visions have I seen!
Methought I was enamoured of an ass.
OBERON There lies your love.
TITANIA How came these things to pass?
80   O, how mine eyes do loathe his visage now!
OBERON Silence awhile.— Robin, take off this head.—
Titania, music call, and strike more dead
Than common sleep of all these five the sense.
TITANIA Music, ho! Music, such as charmeth sleep!

Music, still

85 **ROBIN** Now, when thou wak'st, with thine own fool's
eyes peep.
OBERON Sound, music! Come, my queen, take hands *Oberon and Titania*
with me,   *may dance*
And rock the ground whereon these sleepers be.
Now thou and I are new in amity,
And will tomorrow midnight solemnly
90   Dance in Duke Theseus' house triumphantly,
And bless it to all fair prosperity.
There shall the pairs of faithful lovers be
Wedded, with Theseus, all in jollity.
ROBIN Fairy king, attend, and mark:
95   I do hear the morning lark.
OBERON Then, my queen, in silence sad,
Trip we after the night's shade;
We the globe can compass soon,
Swifter than the wand'ring moon.
100 **TITANIA** Come, my lord, and in our flight
Tell me how it came this night
That I sleeping here was found
With these mortals on the ground.

Exeunt. Sleepers lie still
Wind horns. Enter Theseus, Egeus, Hippolyta, and all his
train

THESEUS Go, one of you, find out the forester,
105   For now our observation is performed;
And since we have the vaward of the day,
My love shall hear the music of my hounds.
Uncouple in the western valley, let them go;

83 these five i.e. Bottom and the lovers   **84 charmeth** brings about by magic   *Music, still* the 'rural
music' may **still** have been playing or perhaps this is a cue for 'still' (i.e. gentle) music; Oberon's **Silence
awhile** may cue the suspension of the former before **Sound, music!** cues the latter   **89 solemnly**
ceremoniously   **90 triumphantly** with great celebration   **94 attend** listen   **96 sad** solemn   **97 Trip** move
swiftly   *his* i.e. Theseus'   **105 observation** observance (of May morning rites)   **106 vaward** vanguard
(i.e. foremost part)   **108 Uncouple** release (pairs of dogs for the hunt)

Dispatch, I say, and find the forester.

[Exit an Attendant]

110   We will, fair queen, up to the mountain's top
And mark the musical confusion
Of hounds and echo in conjunction.

HIPPOLYTA I was with Hercules and Cadmus once,
When in a wood of Crete they bayed the bear
115   With hounds of Sparta; never did I hear
Such gallant chiding, for besides the groves,
The skies, the fountains, every region near
Seemed all one mutual cry. I never heard
So musical a discord, such sweet thunder.

120   **THESEUS** My hounds are bred out of the Spartan kind,
So flewed, so sanded, and their heads are hung
With ears that sweep away the morning dew,
Crook-kneed and dewlapped like Thessalian bulls,
Slow in pursuit, but matched in mouth like bells,
125   Each under each. A cry more tuneable
Was never hallowed to, nor cheered with horn,
In Crete, in Sparta, nor in Thessaly;
Judge when you hear. But, soft! What nymphs are
these?

EGEUS My lord, this is my daughter here asleep,
130   And this, Lysander, this Demetrius is,
This Helena, old Nedar's Helena.
I wonder of their being here together.

THESEUS No doubt they rose up early to observe
The rite of May, and hearing our intent,
135   Came here in grace of our solemnity.
But speak, Egeus; is not this the day
That Hermia should give answer of her choice?

EGEUS It is, my lord.

THESEUS Go, bid the huntsmen wake them with their
horns.

Horns and they wake. Shout within, they all start up.

140   Good morrow, friends. Saint Valentine is past.
Begin these woodbirds but to couple now?

---

113 Cadmus founder of Thebes   **114 bayed** pursued with dogs   **115 hounds of Sparta** dogs famed for their skill   **116 chiding** i.e. barking   **120 kind** breed   **121 so flewed** with the same large cheek folds **sanded** sandy-coloured   **123 dewlapped** with loose folds of skin hanging at the neck   **Thessalian** from Thessaly, an ancient region of north-eastern Greece   **124 matched in mouth** united in barking (i.e. harmonious)   **125 tuneable** melodious   **126 hallowed to** had 'halloo' (a cry of encouragement) shouted to it   **cheered** urged on   **128 soft** wait a moment   **132 of** at   **135 in grace of** to honour   **solemnity** ceremony   **140 Saint Valentine** 14 February, the day on which birds were thought to choose their mates **141 couple** pair off

LYSANDER Pardon, my lord.   *They kneel*
THESEUS I pray you all stand up.   *They stand*
    I know you two are rival enemies.
145 How comes this gentle concord in the world,
    That hatred is so far from jealousy,
    To sleep by hate and fear no enmity?
LYSANDER My lord, I shall reply amazedly,
    Half sleep, half waking. But as yet, I swear,
150 I cannot truly say how I came here.
    But, as I think — for truly would I speak,
    And now I do bethink me, so it is —
    I came with Hermia hither. Our intent
    Was to be gone from Athens, where we might be
155 Without the peril of the Athenian law.
EGEUS Enough, enough, my lord. You have enough;
    I beg the law, the law, upon his head.—
    They would have stolen away, they would, Demetrius,
    Thereby to have defeated you and me:
160 You of your wife and me of my consent,
    Of my consent that she should be your wife.
DEMETRIUS My lord, fair Helen told me of their stealth,
    Of this their purpose hither to this wood,
    And I in fury hither followed them;
165 Fair Helena in fancy followed me.
    But, my good lord, I wot not by what power —
    But by some power it is — my love to Hermia,
    Melted as the snow, seems to me now
    As the remembrance of an idle gaud
170 Which in my childhood I did dote upon.
    And all the faith, the virtue of my heart,
    The object and the pleasure of mine eye,
    Is only Helena. To her, my lord,
    Was I betrothed ere I saw Hermia:
175 But like a sickness did I loathe this food.
    But, as in health, come to my natural taste,
    Now I do wish it, love it, long for it,
    And will for evermore be true to it.
THESEUS Fair lovers, you are fortunately met:
180 Of this discourse we shall hear more anon.
    Egeus, I will overbear your will;
    For in the temple, by and by with us,

146 jealousy suspicion   **159 defeated** frustrated/deprived   **165 fancy** love/infatuation   **169 idle gaud**
worthless trinket   **181 overbear** overrule   **182 by and by** soon

These couples shall eternally be knit.
And, for the morning now is something worn,
185   Our purposed hunting shall be set aside.
Away with us to Athens; three and three,
We'll hold a feast in great solemnity.—
Come, Hippolyta.

Exeunt Duke and lords [and Hippolyta]

DEMETRIUS These things seem small and
    undistinguishable,
190   Like far-off mountains turnèd into clouds.

HERMIA Methinks I see these things with parted eye,
    When everything seems double.

HELENA So methinks:
    And I have found Demetrius like a jewel,
195   Mine own and not mine own.

DEMETRIUS It seems to me
    That yet we sleep, we dream. Do not you think
    The duke was here, and bid us follow him?

HERMIA Yea, and my father.

200 **HELENA** And Hippolyta.

LYSANDER And he bid us follow to the temple.

DEMETRIUS Why, then, we are awake; let's follow him
    And by the way let us recount our dreams.

Exeunt lovers
Bottom wakes

BOTTOM When my cue comes, call me, and I will
205   answer. My next is, 'Most fair Pyramus.' Hey-ho!
    Peter Quince? Flute, the bellows-mender? Snout, the
    tinker? Starveling? God's my life, stolen hence and
    left me asleep! I have had a most rare vision. I had a
    dream, past the wit of man to say what dream it was.
210   Man is but an ass, if he go about to expound this
    dream. Methought I was — there is no man can tell
    what. Methought I was — and methought I had —
    but man is but a patched fool if he will offer to say
    what methought I had. The eye of man hath not
215   heard, the ear of man hath not seen, man's hand is
    not able to taste, his tongue to conceive, nor his
    heart to report, what my dream was. I will get Peter

184 for since **something worn** somewhat spent **185 purposed** intended **187 in** with **solemnity**
ceremony **189 undistinguishable** unrecognizable **191 parted** divided/unfocused **195 Mine ... own**
i.e. because **found**, of uncertain ownership **203 by** on **207 God's** God save **hence** away from here
208 rare unique/marvellous **209 wit** understanding **210 go about** endeavour **213 patched** i.e.
wearing a fool's multicoloured costume **214 The ... was** garbled version of a famous passage about what
the Geneva Bible calls 'the bottom of God's secrets' (1 Corinthians 2:9–10)

Quince to write a ballad of this dream: it shall be
called 'Bottom's Dream', because it hath no bottom;
220   and I will sing it in the latter end of a play, before the
duke. Peradventure, to make it the more gracious, I
shall sing it at her death.   *Exit*

[Act 4 Scene 2]   *running scene 6*

Enter Quince, Flute, Snout and Starveling

QUINCE Have you sent to Bottom's house? Is he come
home yet?

STARVELING He cannot be heard of. Out of doubt he is
transported.

5   FLUTE If he come not, then the play is marred. It goes
not forward, doth it?

QUINCE It is not possible: you have not a man in all
Athens able to discharge Pyramus but he.

FLUTE No, he hath simply the best wit of any handicraft
10   man in Athens.

QUINCE Yea, and the best person too, and he is a very
paramour for a sweet voice.

FLUTE You must say 'paragon'. A paramour is, God bless
us, a thing of naught.

Enter Snug the joiner

15   SNUG Masters, the duke is coming from the temple, and
there is two or three lords and ladies more married. If
our sport had gone forward, we had all been made
men.

FLUTE O sweet bully Bottom! Thus hath he lost sixpence
20   a day during his life; he could not have scaped
sixpence a day. An the duke had not given him
sixpence a day for playing Pyramus, I'll be hanged.
He would have deserved it. Sixpence a day in
Pyramus, or nothing.

Enter Bottom

25   BOTTOM Where are these lads? Where are these hearts?

QUINCE Bottom! O most courageous day! O most happy
hour!

---

219 **bottom** foundation/(is) unfathomable   221 **Peradventure** perhaps   222 **her** presumably Thisbe's
4.2 *Location: Athens*   4 **transported** carried off/transformed   6 **forward** ahead   8 **discharge** perform
9 **wit** intellect   11 **person** appearance, bearing   12 **paramour** malapropism for 'paragon'   14 **naught** i.e.
wickedness, shame (with possible vaginal connotations)   17 **we … men** i.e. our fortunes would have been
made   19 **sixpence a day** i.e. as a reward from the duke (a considerable sum, half a day's wage)
20 **scaped** escaped, avoided   21 **An** if   25 **hearts** fine friends

BOTTOM Masters, I am to discourse wonders: but ask me
not what, for if I tell you, I am no true Athenian. I
30   will tell you everything as it fell out.

QUINCE Let us hear, sweet Bottom.

BOTTOM Not a word of me. All that I will tell you is that
the duke hath dined. Get your apparel together, good
strings to your beards, new ribbons to your pumps.
35   Meet presently at the palace, every man look o'er his
part, for the short and the long is, our play is
preferred. In any case, let Thisbe have clean linen,
and let not him that plays the lion pare his nails, for
they shall hang out for the lion's claws. And, most
40   dear actors, eat no onions nor garlic, for we are to
utter sweet breath, and I do not doubt but to hear
them say, it is a sweet comedy. No more words:
away! Go, away!   *Exeunt*

Act 5 Scene 1   *running scene 7*

Enter Theseus, Hippolyta, Egeus, and his lords

HIPPOLYTA 'Tis strange, my Theseus, that these lovers
speak of.

THESEUS More strange than true. I never may believe
These antic fables, nor these fairy toys.
Lovers and madmen have such seething brains,
5   Such shaping fantasies that apprehend
More than cool reason ever comprehends.
The lunatic, the lover and the poet
Are of imagination all compact.
One sees more devils than vast hell can hold;
10   That is the madman. The lover, all as frantic,
Sees Helen's beauty in a brow of Egypt.
The poet's eye, in a fine frenzy rolling,
Doth glance from heaven to earth, from earth to
heaven,
And as imagination bodies forth
15   The forms of things unknown, the poet's pen
Turns them to shapes and gives to airy nothing

30 **fell out** happened   32 **of** from   34 **strings** i.e. with which to attach the beards   **pumps** light shoes   35 **presently** at once   37 **preferred** recommended   38 **pare** trim   5.1 *his* i.e. Theseus'   1 **that** that which   3 **antic** bizarre/grotesque, with pun on 'antique', antiquated, which is the Quarto spelling   **fairy toys** foolish stories about fairies   5 **shaping** creative   **apprehend** grasp (intellectually)   8 **compact** composed   10 **frantic** mad, frenzied   11 **Helen's** Helen of Troy's   **brow of Egypt** dark-skinned complexion (thought unattractive)   14 **bodies forth** gives shape to

A local habitation and a name.
Such tricks hath strong imagination,
That if it would but apprehend some joy,
20   It comprehends some bringer of that joy.
Or in the night, imagining some fear,
How easy is a bush supposed a bear!

HIPPOLYTA But all the story of the night told over,
And all their minds transfigured so together,
25   More witnesseth than fancy's images
And grows to something of great constancy;
But howsoever, strange and admirable.

Enter lovers: Lysander, Demetrius, Hermia, Helena

THESEUS Here come the lovers, full of joy and mirth.
Joy, gentle friends! Joy and fresh days of love
30   Accompany your hearts!

LYSANDER More than to us
Wait in your royal walks, your board, your bed!

THESEUS Come now, what masques, what dances shall
        we have,
To wear away this long age of three hours
35   Between our after-supper and bedtime?
Where is our usual manager of mirth?
What revels are in hand? Is there no play
To ease the anguish of a torturing hour?
Call Egeus.

40   **EGEUS** Here, mighty Theseus.

THESEUS Say, what abridgement have you for this
        evening?
What masque? What music? How shall we beguile
The lazy time, if not with some delight?

EGEUS There is a brief how many sports are ripe:
45   Make choice of which your highness will see first.

Egeus gives a paper to Lysander

LYSANDER 'The battle with the Centaurs, to be sung   *Reads*
By an Athenian eunuch to the harp.'

THESEUS We'll none of that. That have I told my love,
In glory of my kinsman Hercules.

---

19 apprehend conceive **20 comprehends** incorporates **24 transfigured** changed, affected **25 More witnesseth** is more certain testimony **26 constancy** consistency, truth **27 admirable** wondrous, extraordinary **32 board** table **33 masques** courtly entertainments involving music, dancing and elaborate costumes **35 after-supper** time after the evening meal **41 abridgement** pastime (to shorten the evening) **44 brief** summary **ripe** fully prepared **46 battle ... Centaurs** probably derived from Ovid's *Metamorphoses*, which tells of the battle of the Centaurs and the Lapithae; some versions say that **Hercules** was present

50	LYSANDER 'The riot of the tipsy Bacchanals,	*Reads*
	Tearing the Thracian singer in their rage.'	
	THESEUS That is an old device, and it was played	
	When I from Thebes came last a conqueror.	
	LYSANDER 'The thrice three Muses mourning for the	*Reads*
	death	
55	Of learning, late deceased in beggary.'	
	THESEUS That is some satire, keen and critical,	
	Not sorting with a nuptial ceremony.	
	LYSANDER 'A tedious brief scene of young Pyramus	*Reads*
	And his love Thisbe; very tragical mirth.'	
60	THESEUS Merry and tragical? Tedious and brief?	
	That is, hot ice and wondrous strange snow.	
	How shall we find the concord of this discord?	
	EGEUS A play there is, my lord, some ten words long,	
	Which is as brief as I have known a play;	
65	But by ten words, my lord, it is too long,	
	Which makes it tedious. For in all the play	
	There is not one word apt, one player fitted.	
	And tragical, my noble lord, it is,	
	For Pyramus therein doth kill himself.	
70	Which, when I saw rehearsed, I must confess,	
	Made mine eyes water, but more merry tears	
	The passion of loud laughter never shed.	
	THESEUS What are they that do play it?	
	EGEUS Hard-handed men that work in Athens here,	
75	Which never laboured in their minds till now;	
	And now have toiled their unbreathed memories	
	With this same play, against your nuptial.	
	THESEUS And we will hear it.	
	EGEUS No, my noble lord,	
80	It is not for you. I have heard it over,	
	And it is nothing, nothing in the world;	
	Unless you can find sport in their intents,	
	Extremely stretched and conned with cruel pain,	
	To do you service.	
85	THESEUS I will hear that play.	
	For never anything can be amiss,	

50 riot ... rage another tale from Ovid's *Metamorphoses* in which Orpheus was torn apart by female followers of Bacchus (Roman god of wine)   52 device show   54 thrice ... beggary possible reference to Spenser's poem 'The Tears of the Muses'   56 critical judgemental   57 sorting with appropriate for
61 strange snow a word may be missing here, e.g. 'strange black snow'   62 concord harmony
67 fitted suitable, apt   76 toiled exhausted, taxed   unbreathed unpractised, inexperienced   77 against in preparation for   83 conned learned

When simpleness and duty tender it.
Go, bring them in.— And take your places, ladies.
                                        [*Exit Egeus*]
HIPPOLYTA I love not to see wretchedness o'er-charged
90   And duty in his service perishing.
THESEUS Why, gentle sweet, you shall see no such thing.
HIPPOLYTA He says they can do nothing in this kind.
THESEUS The kinder we, to give them thanks for nothing.
     Our sport shall be to take what they mistake;
95   And what poor duty cannot do, noble respect
     Takes it in might, not merit.
     Where I have come, great clerks have purposèd
     To greet me with premeditated welcomes;
     Where I have seen them shiver and look pale,
100 Make periods in the midst of sentences,
     Throttle their practised accent in their fears,
     And in conclusion dumbly have broke off,
     Not paying me a welcome. Trust me, sweet,
     Out of this silence yet I picked a welcome.
105 And in the modesty of fearful duty
     I read as much as from the rattling tongue
     Of saucy and audacious eloquence.
     Love, therefore, and tongue-tied simplicity
     In least speak most, to my capacity.
     [*Enter Egeus*]
110 **EGEUS** So please your grace, the Prologue is addressed.
     THESEUS Let him approach.   *Flourish* [*of*] *trumpets*
     Enter the Prologue: Quince
     PROLOGUE [QUINCE] If we offend, it is with our good will.
        That you should think, we come not to offend,
        But with good will. To show our simple skill,
115   That is the true beginning of our end.
        Consider then, we come but in despite.
        We do not come as minding to content you,
        Our true intent is. All for your delight
        We are not here. That you should here repent you,

---

87 **simpleness** unassuming simplicity   89 **wretchedness o'er-charged** humble people overburdened
90 **his service** its attempt to serve   92 **kind** respect   94 **take** accept, comprehend, value   95 **noble
respect** dignity and consideration that comes with nobility   96 **in . . . merit** in terms of effort rather than
actual value   97 **clerks** scholars   100 **Make periods** full stops/rhetorical pauses   101 **accent** speech,
intonation   104 **picked** extracted, detected   105 **modesty** propriety/shyness   **fearful** frightened
109 **capacity** understanding   110 **addressed** ready   112 **will.** Quince inadvertently inserts a full stop
here and changes the meaning of the line   114 **will.** another misplaced full stop   115 **end** aim
116 **despite** malice   **we . . . you** correctly punctuated, this would read 'we come – but in despite we do not
come – as minding to content you'   118 **is.** erroneous full stop   **All** exclusively   **delight** missing
punctuation (e.g. full stop, semi-colon)   119 **here.** erroneous full stop

120   The actors are at hand; and by their show,
        You shall know all that you are like to know.
        THESEUS This fellow doth not stand upon points.
        LYSANDER He hath rid his prologue like a rough colt: he
        knows not the stop. A good moral, my lord. It is not
125   enough to speak, but to speak true.
        HIPPOLYTA Indeed he hath played on his prologue like a
        child on a recorder: a sound, but not in government.
        THESEUS His speech was like a tangled chain: nothing
        impaired, but all disordered. Who is next?
        Enter, with a trumpet[er] before them, Pyramus [Bottom]
        and Thisbe [Flute], Wall [Snout], Moonshine [Starveling]
        and Lion [Snug]
130   PROLOGUE [QUINCE] Gentles, perchance you wonder at
                this show,
        But wonder on, till truth make all things plain.
        This man is Pyramus, if you would know;
        This beauteous lady Thisbe is certain.
        This man with lime and rough-cast doth present
135   Wall, that vile Wall which did these lovers sunder.
        And through Wall's chink, poor souls, they are content
        To whisper. At the which let no man wonder.
        This man, with lantern, dog, and bush of thorn,
        Presenteth Moonshine. For, if you will know,
140   By moonshine did these lovers think no scorn
        To meet at Ninus' tomb, there, there to woo.
        This grisly beast, which Lion hight by name,
        The trusty Thisbe, coming first by night,
        Did scare away, or rather did affright.
145   And as she fled, her mantle she did fall,
        Which Lion vile with bloody mouth did stain.
        Anon comes Pyramus, sweet youth and tall,
        And finds his trusty Thisbe's mantle slain;
        Whereat, with blade, with bloody blameful blade,
150   He bravely broached his boiling bloody breast.
        And Thisbe, tarrying in mulberry shade,
        His dagger drew, and died. For all the rest,
        Let Lion, Moonshine, Wall, and lovers twain

---

120 show appearance/performance   **121 like** likely   **122 stand upon points** dwell on trivialities/insist on
(correct) punctuation   **123 rid** dispensed with/ridden   **rough** untrained   **124 stop** pulling-up (of a horse)/
full stop   **127 government** control   **128 nothing** not   **135 sunder** separate   **140 scorn** shame, disdain
142 hight is called   **145 mantle** loose cloak   **fall** let fall   **147 tall** fine/brave   **150 broached** pierced
153 twain two/separated

At large discourse, while here they do remain.

Exeunt all but Wall

155   THESEUS I wonder if the lion be to speak.

DEMETRIUS No wonder, my lord: one lion may, when many asses do.

WALL [SNOUT] In this same interlude it doth befall
That I, one Snout by name, present a wall.
160   And such a wall, as I would have you think,
That had in it a crannied hole or chink,
Through which the lovers, Pyramus and Thisbe,
Did whisper often, very secretly.
This loam, this rough-cast and this stone doth show
165   That I am that same wall; the truth is so.
And this the cranny is, right and sinister,   *Gestures to gap*
Through which the fearful lovers are to whisper.   *between his legs*

THESEUS Would you desire lime and hair to speak better?

170   DEMETRIUS It is the wittiest partition that ever I heard discourse, my lord.

THESEUS Pyramus draws near the wall. Silence!

Enter Pyramus

PYRAMUS [BOTTOM] O grim-looked night! O night with hue so black!
O night, which ever art when day is not!
175   O night, O night! Alack, alack, alack,
I fear my Thisbe's promise is forgot.
And thou, O wall, thou sweet and lovely wall
That stands between her father's ground and mine!
Thou wall, O wall, O sweet and lovely wall,
180   Show me thy chink, to blink through with mine
eyne!   *Wall opens his legs*
Thanks, courteous wall. Jove shield thee well for
this.   *Pyramus peers between Wall's legs*
But what see I? No Thisbe do I see.
O wicked wall, through whom I see no bliss!
Cursed be thy stones for thus deceiving me!

185   THESEUS The wall, methinks, being sensible, should
curse again.

PYRAMUS [BOTTOM] No, in truth, sir, he should not.
'Deceiving me' is Thisbe's cue; she is to enter and I

---

158 **interlude** short play   166 **sinister** left   167 **fearful** frightened   170 **partition** wall/section of a scholarly book   173 **grim-looked** grim-looking, forbidding   180 **chink** plays on sense of 'vagina/anus'   181 **Jove** Roman supreme god   184 **stones** plays on sense of 'testicles'   185 **sensible** capable of feeling **again** in response

am to spy her through the wall. You shall see, it will
fall pat as I told you. Yonder she comes.

Enter Thisbe

190 **THISBE [FLUTE]** O wall, full often hast thou heard my
                moans,

       For parting my fair Pyramus and me.
       My cherry lips have often kissed thy stones,
       Thy stones with lime and hair knit up in thee.

       PYRAMUS [BOTTOM] I see a voice; now will I to the chink,

195   To spy an I can hear my Thisbe's face. Thisbe?
       THISBE [FLUTE] My love thou art, my love I think.
       PYRAMUS [BOTTOM] Think what thou wilt, I am thy
                lover's grace

       And like Limander am I trusty still.

       THISBE [FLUTE] And I like Helen, till the Fates me kill.

200   **PYRAMUS [BOTTOM]** Not Shafalus to Procrus was so true.
       THISBE [FLUTE] As Shafalus to Procrus, I to you.
       PYRAMUS [BOTTOM] O, kiss me through the hole of
                this vile wall!

       THISBE [FLUTE] I kiss the wall's hole, not your lips at all.
       PYRAMUS [BOTTOM] Wilt thou at Ninny's tomb meet
                me straightway?

205   **THISBE [FLUTE]** 'Tide life, 'tide death, I come without
                delay.   [*Exeunt Pyramus and Thisbe*]

       WALL [SNOUT] Thus have I, Wall, my part dischargèd so;
       And, being done, thus Wall away doth go.   *Exit*

       THESEUS Now is the mural down between the two
       neighbours.

210   **DEMETRIUS** No remedy, my lord, when walls are so
       wilful to hear without warning.

       HIPPOLYTA This is the silliest stuff that e'er I heard.

       THESEUS The best in this kind are but shadows, and the
       worst are no worse, if imagination amend them.

215   **HIPPOLYTA** It must be your imagination then, and not
       theirs.

       THESEUS If we imagine no worse of them than they of
       themselves, they may pass for excellent men. Here
       come two noble beasts in, a man and a lion.

189 pat exactly   **193 lime** probably pronounced 'limb', thus playing on sense of 'penis'   **hair** plays on
'pubic hair'   **195 an** if   **196 My ... love** Thisbe misplaces the pause that should be after 'My love'
197 lover's grace i.e. gracious lover   **198 Limander** malapropism for 'Leander', lover of Hero   **199 Helen**
mistake for 'Hero'   **200 Shafalus to Procrus** mistakes for 'Cephalus', who was married to 'Procris'
203 hole plays on 'arsehole'   **205 'Tide** betide, i.e. come   **208 mural** wall   **210 walls ... hear** derived
from the proverb 'walls have ears'   **wilful** willing   **213 in this kind** of this sort   **shadows** images/
reflections/actors

Enter Lion and Moonshine [with a lantern, thorn-bush and dog]

220   **LION [SNUG]** You, ladies, you, whose gentle hearts do fear
        The smallest monstrous mouse that creeps on floor,
        May now perchance both quake and tremble here,
        When lion rough in wildest rage doth roar.
        Then know that I, one Snug the joiner, am
225   A lion fell, nor else no lion's dam,
        For if I should as lion come in strife
        Into this place, 'twere pity on my life.

      THESEUS A very gentle beast, and of a good conscience.

      DEMETRIUS The very best at a beast, my lord, that e'er I
230   saw.

      LYSANDER This lion is a very fox for his valour.

      THESEUS True, and a goose for his discretion.

      DEMETRIUS Not so, my lord, for his valour cannot carry
        his discretion, and the fox carries the goose.

235   **THESEUS** His discretion, I am sure, cannot carry his
        valour, for the goose carries not the fox. It is well.
        Leave it to his discretion, and let us hearken to the
        moon.

      MOONSHINE [STARVELING] This lantern doth the
        hornèd moon present—

240   **DEMETRIUS** He should have worn the horns on his head.

      THESEUS He is no crescent, and his horns are invisible
        within the circumference.

      MOONSHINE [STARVELING] This lantern doth the hornèd
        moon present:
        Myself the man i'th'moon doth seem to be.

245   **THESEUS** This is the greatest error of all the rest; the man
        should be put into the lantern. How is it else the man
        i'th'moon?

      DEMETRIUS He dares not come there for the candle. For
        you see it is already in snuff.

250   **HIPPOLYTA** I am aweary of this moon; would he would
        change!

---

221 **monstrous** frightening/enormous   223 **rough** wild/cruel   225 **fell** fierce   **dam** mother   229 **at** i.e. at playing   **beast** puns on best   231 **a very fox** i.e. cunning   **for** i.e. for all   232 **goose ... discretion** i.e. foolish   **discretion** judgement/prudence   234 **carries** i.e. literally, as prey   239 **hornèd** i.e. crescent-shaped   240 **horns ... head** i.e. as a cuckold (men with unfaithful wives were said to grow horns)   241 **no crescent** no growing moon (presumably because he is so thin)   249 **in snuff** in need of blowing out/angry

THESEUS It appears, by his small light of discretion, that
    he is in the wane. But yet, in courtesy, in all reason,
    we must stay the time.
255 LYSANDER Proceed, Moon.
MOONSHINE [STARVELING] All that I have to say is to
    tell you that the lantern is the moon; I, the man in
    the moon; this thorn-bush, my thorn-bush; and this
    dog, my dog.
260 DEMETRIUS Why, all these should be in the lantern, for
    they are in the moon. But silence — here comes
    Thisbe.
Enter Thisbe
THISBE [FLUTE] This is old Ninny's tomb. Where is my
    love?
LION [SNUG] O!
The lion roars. Thisbe runs off [dropping her mantle]
265 DEMETRIUS Well roared, Lion.
THESEUS Well run, Thisbe.
HIPPOLYTA Well shone, Moon. Truly, the moon shines
    with a good grace.
                [Lion shakes Thisbe's mantle, and exits]
THESEUS Well moused, Lion.
270 DEMETRIUS And then came Pyramus.
LYSANDER And so the lion vanished.
Enter Pyramus
PYRAMUS [BOTTOM] Sweet Moon, I thank thee for thy
    sunny beams,
    I thank thee, Moon, for shining now so bright,
    For by thy gracious, golden, glittering gleams,
275   I trust to taste of truest Thisbe sight.
          But stay, O spite!
          But mark, poor knight,
          What dreadful dole is here?
          Eyes, do you see?
280   How can it be?
          O dainty duck! O dear!
          Thy mantle good,
          What, stained with blood!
          Approach, you Furies fell!
285   O Fates, come, come,

---

253 **in the wane** decreasing/lacking   **reason** i.e. reasonable behaviour   254 **stay the time** wait for the
moment, sit it out   269 **moused** seized/shaken (refers to **Thisbe's mantle**)   278 **dole** sorrow, grievous
occurrence   284 **Furies** three classical goddesses of vengeance   **fell** fierce   285 **Fates** three classical
goddesses in control of human destiny (a thread which would be cut when death was due)

Cut thread and thrum,
Quail, crush, conclude, and quell!

THESEUS This passion, and the death of a dear friend,
would go near to make a man look sad.

290 **HIPPOLYTA** Beshrew my heart, but I pity the man.

PYRAMUS [BOTTOM] O wherefore, Nature, didst thou
lions frame?
Since lion vile hath here deflowered my dear:
Which is — no, no — which was the fairest dame
That lived, that loved, that liked, that looked
with cheer.

295　　　Come, tears, confound:
Out, sword, and wound
The pap of Pyramus,
Ay, that left pap,
Where heart doth hop:

300　　　Thus die I, thus, thus, thus.　　　　　*Stabs himself*
Now am I dead,
Now am I fled,
My soul is in the sky.
Tongue, lose thy light,

305　　　Moon take thy flight,　　　[*Exit Moonshine*]
Now die, die, die, die, die.　　　　　*Dies*

DEMETRIUS No die, but an ace for him; for he is but one.

LYSANDER Less than an ace, man: for he is dead, he is
nothing.

310 **THESEUS** With the help of a surgeon he might yet
recover, and prove an ass.

HIPPOLYTA How chance Moonshine is gone before
Thisbe comes back and finds her lover?

Enter Thisbe

THESEUS She will find him by starlight. Here she comes,
315　　and her passion ends the play.

HIPPOLYTA Methinks she should not use a long one for
such a Pyramus: I hope she will be brief.

DEMETRIUS A mote will turn the balance, which
Pyramus, which Thisbe, is the better.

320 **LYSANDER** She hath spied him already with those sweet
eyes.

286 **thrum** end of warp-thread on a weaving loom, i.e. everything　287 **Quail** end, destroy　**quell** overcome, ruin　288 **passion** fit of grief　**friend** lover　289 **go near to** almost　290 **Beshrew** curse　291 **frame** create　292 **deflowered** presumably Bottom's mistake for 'devoured'　294 **cheer** face/joy　297 **pap** breast (usually a woman's)　304 **Tongue** error for 'eye'　307 **die** one of a pair of dice　**ace** one (single spot on a die)　311 **ass** puns on ace　315 **passion** sorrow/suffering (resulting in death)　316 **long one** i.e. fit of grief　318 **mote** tiny particle

DEMETRIUS And thus she means, *videlicet*—
THISBE [FLUTE] Asleep, my love?
              What, dead, my dove?
325   O Pyramus, arise!
              Speak, speak. Quite dumb?
              Dead, dead? A tomb
              Must cover thy sweet eyes.
              These lily lips,
330   This cherry nose,
              These yellow cowslip cheeks,
              Are gone, are gone!
              Lovers, make moan:
              His eyes were green as leeks.
335   O Sisters Three,
              Come, come to me,
              With hands as pale as milk.
              Lay them in gore,
              Since you have shore
340   With shears his thread of silk.
              Tongue, not a word.
              Come, trusty sword,
              Come, blade, my breast imbrue.   *Stabs herself*
              And farewell friends,
345   Thus Thisbe ends:
              Adieu, adieu, adieu.   *Dies*
THESEUS Moonshine and Lion are left to bury the dead.
DEMETRIUS Ay, and Wall too.
BOTTOM No, I assure you, the wall is down that parted   *Gets up*
350   their fathers. Will it please you to see the epilogue, or
to hear a Bergamasque dance between two of our
company?
THESEUS No epilogue, I pray you, for your play needs no
excuse. Never excuse; for when the players are all
355   dead, there need none to be blamed. Marry, if he that
writ it had played Pyramus and hung himself in
Thisbe's garter, it would have been a fine tragedy:
and so it is, truly, and very notably discharged. But
come, your Bergamasque; let your epilogue alone.   *A dance*
360   The iron tongue of midnight hath told twelve.
Lovers, to bed, 'tis almost fairy time.

322 **means** laments/intends   *videlicet* 'that is to say' (Latin)   335 **Sisters Three** i.e. the Fates
339 **shore** shorn, cut   340 **thread of silk** i.e. life   343 **imbrue** pierce   351 **Bergamasque dance** rustic
dance, named after the people of Bergamo, Italy   **between** i.e. performed by   360 **iron tongue** clapper of a
bell   **told** counted, i.e. rung (puns on 'tolled')

I fear we shall out-sleep the coming morn
As much as we this night have overwatched.
This palpable-gross play hath well beguiled
365   The heavy gait of night. Sweet friends, to bed.
A fortnight hold we this solemnity,
In nightly revels and new jollity.   *Exeunt*

Enter [Robin] Puck   **With a broom**

ROBIN Now the hungry lion roars,
And the wolf beholds the moon.
370   Whilst the heavy ploughman snores,
All with weary task fordone.
Now the wasted brands do glow,
Whilst the screech-owl, screeching loud,
Puts the wretch that lies in woe
375   In remembrance of a shroud.
Now it is the time of night
That the graves all gaping wide,
Every one lets forth his sprite,
In the church-way paths to glide.
380   And we fairies that do run
By the triple Hecate's team,
From the presence of the sun,
Following darkness like a dream,
Now are frolic; not a mouse
385   Shall disturb this hallowed house.
I am sent with broom before,
To sweep the dust behind the door.

Enter King and Queen of Fairies [Oberon and Titania]
with their train

OBERON Through the house give glimmering light,
By the dead and drowsy fire,
390   Every elf and fairy sprite
Hop as light as bird from briar,
And this ditty, after me,
Sing, and dance it trippingly.

---

363 overwatched stayed up late   364 palpable-gross obviously clumsy   beguiled whiled away
365 heavy gait slow/sleepy passage   366 solemnity celebration   370 heavy exhausted   371 fordone
worn out   372 wasted brands burnt logs   373 screech-owl the barn owl's cry was thought to be a bad
omen   378 sprite spirit   381 triple Hecate classical goddess of witchcraft and night, associated with the
moon; often represented in triple form, she was known as Luna/Cynthia in heaven, Diana on earth, and
Proserpina in the underworld   team i.e. the creatures, probably dragons, pulling her chariot   384 frolic
frolicsome, merry   385 hallowed blessed   387 behind out from behind/behind   388 give glimmering
light probably a command to the fairies, who may have candles with them (perhaps carried on their heads to
leave their hands free for dancing)   393 trippingly skilfully, lightly

TITANIA First, rehearse this song by rote,
395   To each word a warbling note.
          Hand in hand, with fairy grace,
          Will we sing and bless this place.
[FAIRIES *sing*]   *The Song*   *Fairies dance*
          Now until the break of day
          Through this house each fairy stray.
400   To the best bride-bed will we,
          Which by us shall blessèd be.
          And the issue there create
          Ever shall be fortunate.
          So shall all the couples three
405   Ever true in loving be.
          And the blots of Nature's hand
          Shall not in their issue stand.
          Never mole, hare-lip, nor scar,
          Nor mark prodigious, such as are
410   Despisèd in nativity,
          Shall upon their children be.
          With this field-dew consecrate,
          Every fairy take his gait,
          And each several chamber bless,
415   Through this palace, with sweet peace.
          Ever shall in safety rest,
          And the owner of it blest.
          Trip away, make no stay;
          Meet me all by break of day.
                    [*Exeunt all but Robin*]
420 ROBIN If we shadows have offended,
          Think but this, and all is mended,
          That you have but slumbered here
          While these visions did appear.
          And this weak and idle theme,
425   No more yielding but a dream,
          Gentles, do not reprehend.
          If you pardon, we will mend.
          And, as I am an honest Puck,
          If we have unearnèd luck
430   Now to scape the serpent's tongue,

394 rehearse recite   rote heart   400 best bride-bed i.e. that of Theseus and Hippolyta   402 issue children   create created   409 prodigious ominous   412 consecrate holy, blessed   413 gait (own) course   414 several individual   418 stay delay   424 weak deficient   idle foolish/trifling   425 yielding but meaningful than   426 Gentles ladies and gentlemen   reprehend reprove   427 mend improve, put it right   430 serpent's tongue i.e. audience hisses

We will make amends ere long:
Else the Puck a liar call.
So, goodnight unto you all.
Give me your hands, if we be friends,
435   And Robin shall restore amends.

---

434 Give ... **hands** i.e. applaud   **435 restore amends** make amends in return

TEXTUAL NOTES

Q = First Quarto text of 1600
F = First Folio text of 1623
F2 = a correction introduced in the Second Folio text of 1632
F4 = a correction introduced in the Fourth Folio text of 1685
Ed = a correction introduced by a later editor
SD = stage direction
SH = speech heading (i.e. speaker's name)

List of parts = Ed

1.1.7 nights = F. Q = night **10 New-bent** = Ed. F = Now bent **25 Stand forth, Demetrius** = Ed. *Set in italic as a stage direction in* F **27 Stand forth, Lysander** = Ed. *Set in italic as a stage direction in* F **134 Ay me, for** = Q. F = For **I could ever** = Q. F = ever I could **138 low** = Ed. F = loue **142 eyes** = Q. F = eie **145 momentary** = F's *modernization of* Q's momentany **161 removed** = F. Q = remote **169 to** = Q. F = for **175 love** = F. Q = loves **185 your** = Q. F = you **203 none** = F. Q = no fault **208 like** = F. Q = as **210 into** = F. Q = unto a **219 sweet** = Ed. F = sweld **228 dote** = Q. F = dotes **242 often** = F. Q = so oft **251 this** = Q. F = his

1.2.10 grow on to = F. Q = grow to **40 You must** = F. Q = Flute, you must **62 if it be** = Q. F = if be **77 roar** = F. Q = roare you **95 will we** = Q. F = we will

2.1.1 SH ROBIN = Ed. F = *Rob. Sometimes* Pucke **5 thorough flood, thorough** = Q. F = through flood, through **33 sprite** = Q. F = spirit **34 not you he** = Q. F = you not hee **47 filly** = Q. F = silly **62 SH TITANIA** = Ed. F = *Qu.* **Fairies** = Ed. F = Fairy **66 hast** = Q. F = wast **70 step** = Q. F = steepe **78 not thou** = Q. F = thou not **80 Aegles** = Ed. F = Eagles **81 Antiopa** = Q. F = *Atiopa* **92 petty** = F. Q = pelting **108 hoary-headed** = Q1. F = hoared headed **110 thin** = Ed. F = chin **138 do I** = Q. F = I doe **158 saw** = Q. F = say **178 round about** = Q. F = about **214 do use** = Q. F = doe **242 the field** = Q. F = and Field **247 I'll** = Q. F = I

2.2.9 SH FIRST FAIRY = Ed. *Not in* F **13, 24 SH CHORUS** = Ed. *Not in* F **14 our** = Q. F = your **35 wood** = Q. F = woods **48 we can** = Q. F = can you **49 interchainèd** = Q. F = interchanged **67 found** = Q. F = finde **68 On** = Q. F = One **104 shows her art** = Ed. F = her shewes art. Q = shewes art. **113 Helena now I** = F. Q = Helena I **140 they** = Q. F = that **149 ate** = Ed. *Spelled* eate *in* F **150 you** = Q. F = yet

3.1.28 yourselves = F. Q = your selfe **43 them** = Q. F = him **48 SH SNOUT** = Ed. Q/F = Sn., *which could be* SNOUT *or* SNUG. F2 = SNUG. **51 SD [*Robin may*] enter** = Ed. F = *Enter Pucke. Not in* Q **73 SD *Robin* [*may*] enter** = Ed. Q/F = *Enter Robin* **79 SH PYRAMUS [BOTTOM]** = Ed. F = *Pir.* **86 SH THISBE [FLUTE]** = Ed. F = *This.* **99 SD *Enter … head** placed ten lines later in* F *at a possible re-entry point for Bottom* **124 with** = Q. F = and **137 On … thee** = Q. F *prints before the two preceding lines* **157 Peaseblossom … Mustardseed!** *set as SD in* F **158 SH PEASEBLOSSOM** = Ed. F = *Fai.* **159 SH COBWEB** = Ed. *Not in* F **160 SH MOTH** = Ed. *Not in* F **161 SH MUSTARDSEED** = Ed. *Not in* F **162 SH ALL** = Ed. *Not in* F **174 SH PEASEBLOSSOM** = Ed. F = *1.Fai.* **175 SH COBWEB** = Ed. *Not in* F. **176 SH**

MOTH = Ed. F = *2.Fai.* **177 SH MUSTARDSEED** = Ed. F = *3.Fai.* **187 you of** = Q. F = of you **189 Mustardseed.** F *here accidentally repeats 'Peas. Pease-blossome.'* **194 you of** = Ed. F = you **198 weeps, weeps** = Q. F = weepes, weepe

3.2.5 haunted = Q. F = gaunted **58 murdered** = Q. F = murderer **68 tell true** = Q. F *omits repetition* **80 I so** = Ed. F = I **85 sleep** = Ed. F = slip **121 SD [***following***]** = Ed. F = *and* **123 come** = Q. F = comes **145 all are** = Q. F = are all **151 were men** = Q. F = are men **167 till** = Q. F = to **172 is it** = Q. F = it is **174 Helen, it** = Q. F = It **176 abide** = F*'s modernization of* Q*'s* aby **183 thy sound** = Q. F = that sound **214 like** = Ed, F = life **221 passionate** = F. *Not in* Q **244 my** = Q. F = mine **252 prayers** = Ed. F = praise **261 sir** = F. Q = heele. *Some eds emend to* yield **269 potion** = Q. F = poison **286 of doubt** = F. *Some eds omit* of **347 abide** = F*'s modernization of* Q*'s* aby **359 wilfully** = Q. F = willingly **362 hath** = F. Q = had **387 employ** = Q. F = imply **392 night-swift** = F. Q = nights swift **399 exile** = Q. F = dxile **411 feared** = Ed. F = sear'd **435 SD *shifting places*** *placed five lines earlier in* F **440 now** = Q. *Not in* F **451 sometime** = F. Q = sometimes **467 To your** = Ed. F = your

4.1.5 SH BOTTOM = Ed. F = *Clow.* **10 you your** = Q. F = your **49 favours** = Q. F = savors **73 o'er** = Ed. F = or **80 do loathe his** = Q. F = doth loath this **81 this head** = Q. F = his head **83 five** = Ed. F = fine **85 Now, when** = Q. F = When **91 prosperity** = Q. F = posterity **94 Fairy** = Q. F = Faire **118 Seemed** = F2. F = Seeme **132 their** = Q. F = this **146 is** = Q. F = is is **154 might be** = F. Q = might **165 followed** = F. Q = following **174 saw** = Ed. F = see **177 I do** = Q. F = doe I **180 shall hear more** = F. Q = more will here **192 everything** = Q. F = euery things **196 It seems** = F. Q *precedes with* Are you sure / That we are awake? **201 bid** = F. Q = did bid **218 ballad** = Ed (F4). F = ballet

4.2.0 SD *Flute* = Ed. F = *Flute, Thisbie.* **5 SH FLUTE** = Ed. F = *This.* **14 naught** = F2. F = nought **29 no true** = F. Q = not true **30 everything as** = F. Q = every thing right as

5.1.16 airy = Ed. F = aire **39 Egeus** = F. Q = Philostrate **40 SH EGEUS** = F, *replacing* Q*'s* PHILOSTRATE *throughout this scene* **44 ripe** = Q. F = rife **46 SH LYSANDER** = F. Q *assigns these comments to* THESEUS **79 SH EGEUS** = Ed. F = *Phi., a vestige from the* Q *version of the scene, in which Philostrate serves as the 'manager of mirth'* **111 SH THESEUS** = Q. F = *Duke or Du. throughout scene* **126 his** = F. Q = this **129 SD *with* ... *them*** = Ed. F = *Tawyer with a Trumpet before them (William Tawyer was an actor in Shakespeare's company)* **148 trusty Thisbe's** = Q. F = Thisbies **154 SD *Exeunt* ... *Wall*** F *provides a redundant SD three lines later: 'Exit Lyon, Thisbie, and Moonshine'* **187 enter** = F. Q = enter now **193 up in thee** = F. Q = now againe **199 And I** = Q. F = And **208 mural** = Ed. F = morall. Q = Moon used **212 SH HIPPOLYTA** = Q. F = *Dut. (for Dutchess) throughout* **227 on** = Q. F = of **237 hearken** = F. Q = listen **261 they are** = F. Q = all these are **274 gleams** = Ed. F = beames **275 taste** = F. Q = take **311 prove** = F. Q = yet proove **319 is the better.** = F. Q *continues* better: hee for a man, God warnd us; she for a woman, God blesse us. **349 SH BOTTOM** = F. Q = LYON **368 lion** = Ed. F = Lyons **394 this** = F. Q = your **397 SD *The Song*** = F. *Assigned to* Oberon *in* Q.

SCENE-BY-SCENE ANALYSIS

ACT 1 SCENE 1

Lines 1–129: Theseus and Hippolyta discuss their wedding, measuring the time they must wait by the moon – a key motif in the play. Theseus has defeated Hippolyta in battle, but promises to wed her 'in another key'. Egeus interrupts, bringing his daughter and her two suitors. In formal language, reflecting the court setting, he complains that Demetrius has his permission to marry Hermia, but that she loves Lysander, who has 'bewitched' her, raising the themes of love and magic. Egeus asks for the 'ancient privilege of Athens', whereby Hermia must obey him or be executed. Hermia, subject to patriarchal rule, is reduced to a commodity by Egeus' claim that 'As she is mine, I may dispose of her'. As Hermia argues that Lysander is as 'worthy' as Demetrius, she raises another key motif in the play: the idea that perceptions of 'worth' are often created solely by the desire of others. Theseus rules that Hermia has until his wedding to decide whether to marry Demetrius, 'die the death' or 'endure the livery of a nun' (a futile and 'barren' existence). Hermia shows strength, claiming she will live and die a virgin as she 'consents not to give sovereignty' to Demetrius. Egeus, Lysander and Demetrius argue over Hermia, with Lysander insisting that he is 'as well possessed' as Demetrius, and furthermore that, until recently, 'inconstant' Demetrius courted Helena, who 'dotes' on him. Theseus decrees, however, that he may not 'extenuate' Athens' law.

Lines 130–182: Hermia and Lysander discuss their circumstances. Lysander says that all the evidence of his reading from 'tale or history' shows that 'The course of true love never did run smooth.'

He lists various examples of thwarted love, perhaps implicitly drawing attention to the varied source materials for the play and acknowledging the familiar narrative theme of forbidden love. Hermia agrees to meet Lysander in the woods the next night and run away to his aunt's house where they can marry, safe from 'sharp Athenian law'.

Lines 183–254: Helena wishes she looked like Hermia so that Demetrius would love her. Hermia protests that she does not ask for Demetrius' love, which he gives her even though she curses him, but Helena blames her nonetheless. Hermia and Lysander tell Helena of their planned flight and wish her luck. Once alone, Helena dwells on how she is considered as 'fair' as Hermia throughout Athens, but this does not matter, as Demetrius does not think so. She observes how 'Things base and vile, holding no quantity, / Love can transpose to form and dignity': desire can give something or someone worth. She resolves to tell Demetrius about Hermia and Lysander's intended escape.

ACT 1 SCENE 2

The second group of characters are introduced – the artisans who are to perform as part of the wedding entertainment. Their preparation and performance of the play-within-the-play creates comedy and a clear sense of theatrical self-awareness, as the limitations of their stagecraft highlight the sophistication of the wider play. The position of this scene between one involving the mortals and one involving the fairies perhaps emphasizes the role of the theatre in the movement between reality and illusion.

Quince allocates parts in 'The most lamentable comedy and most cruel death of Pyramus and Thisbe', a humorous muddling of the genres of comedy and tragedy, but a reminder that there is often a fine line between the two. Comedy is created through Bottom's interruptions as he asks to be allowed to play all the parts and demonstrates how good he would be at each. Humour is also created through language – punning, bawdy and Bottom's malapropisms.

The practicalities and politics of staging are touched upon, as they discuss costumes, the fact that Flute does not wish to play a woman since he has 'a beard coming' and how they must not incur the displeasure of their noble audience by frightening the ladies as 'that were enough to hang us all'. They agree to meet the next night in the wood to rehearse 'by moonlight', so as to be private.

ACT 2 SCENE 1

The final group of characters, the fairies, are introduced, and their world is evoked through both natural imagery, suggesting the night-time and woodland, and mythical and expansive language, suggesting a world not subject to the same limitations as the mortal one. Despite the beauty and enchantment they conjure, there is also a potentially chaotic, darker element to their world, contrasting with the restrained and ordered court.

Lines 1–60: Robin Goodfellow (the Puck) and the Fairy establish their roles in the mortal world – either creating the natural environment by tasks such as placing dew as 'a pearl in every cowslip's ear', or mischievously interfering with domestic life – 'knavish' Robin 'frights the maidens' or will 'Mislead night-wanderers, laughing at their harm'. They signal the approach of Oberon and Titania and establish that the king and queen of the fairies are currently arguing over ownership of a 'changeling' Indian boy that Titania has as her attendant.

Lines 61–147: Titania goes to leave, but Oberon orders her to 'tarry', asking 'am not I thy Lord?', showing a similar patriarchal authority to Theseus in the mortal court and emphasizing the parallels between these two characters. Titania describes how their quarrel has impacted on the mortal world, showing the darker side of the fairies, as the land is covered with 'Contagious fogs' and the corn 'Hath rotted'. Oberon argues that Titania could end their quarrel and thus mortal suffering by giving him the little Indian boy, but Titania refuses. Oberon declines Titania's invitation to dance in the fairy round. She leaves.

Lines 148–191: Using imagery that evokes the limitless and enchanted world of the fairies and reinforces the sexual and hunting themes that recur in the play, Oberon describes to Robin a time when he saw Cupid aim an arrow at 'a fair vestal', but hit a flower instead, turning it 'purple with love's wound'. He sends Robin to collect this flower, the juice from which will make the person on whose 'sleeping eyelids' it has been placed fall in love with the first creature they see on waking. Once alone, Oberon reveals his intention to apply the juice to Titania's eyes and watch her fall in love with the first thing she looks at, 'Be it on lion, bear, or wolf or bull'. He will make her 'render up her page' before he will remove the spell. Hearing Helena and Demetrius approach, he declares 'I am invisible' – reinforcing his magical nature, but also drawing attention to theatre and dramatic irony as he, too, becomes an 'audience', invisibly observing the action.

Lines 192–273: Demetrius is angered by the difficulty in finding his way, claiming that it makes him 'wood' (mad or frantic), emphasizing the disorder associated with this setting. He tries to stop Helena following him, telling her that he does not love her and warning that she is risking 'the rich worth' of her virginity by entering the woods with him. Helena acknowledges his power over her by describing herself as his 'spaniel', that he may 'beat' and 'spurn', although this passivity contrasts with her assertive warning that she will follow him wherever he goes. When they have gone, Robin returns with the flower and Oberon takes some of it to 'streak' the eyes of Titania, then sends Robin to apply some to 'disdainful' Demetrius – whom he will know by his 'Athenian garments' – so that he will love Helena.

ACT 2 SCENE 2

The rapid action of the next few scenes highlights the confusion caused by the fairies' involvement in the mortal world and the disorientating nature of the dark woods.

Lines 1–34: Titania calls her train to sing her to sleep before they go about their fairy tasks. Once she is asleep, Oberon squeezes the flower's juice onto her eyelids and leaves.

Lines 35–83: Lysander and Hermia are lost and decide to rest until daylight. Lysander wishes to sleep close to Hermia, but she asks him, out of 'love and courtesy' to 'Lie further off', as this is more fitting to her virtue. Robin the Puck enters, complaining that he has searched the forest for an Athenian and 'found none'. He sees sleeping Lysander in his Athenian clothes, and Hermia lying at a distance. Assuming that Hermia is distanced because the man is a 'lack-love' who has spurned her, he concludes that these are the mortals that Oberon described. He applies the juice to Lysander's eyelids and leaves as Demetrius enters, running away from Helena.

Lines 84–156: Helena pleads with Demetrius to stop but he refuses and runs off, leaving her alone in the dark. In a speech that makes reference to sight, drawing attention to the way the characters' literal and metaphorical perception is distorted by both magic and love, she reveals her jealousy of Hermia and her 'blessèd and attractive eyes'. Helena bewails her own appearance, claiming that she is 'ugly as a bear' and that Demetrius sees her 'as a monster'. She stumbles on Lysander and wakes him. On seeing her, enchanted Lysander falls in love and rejects Hermia, saying that Helena is 'the worthier maid'. Helena, convinced that Lysander is mocking her, leaves. He follows, leaving 'hated' Hermia alone. Hermia wakes from a nightmare, the description of which highlights the more potentially threatening side of the wood and the fairies, as she finds herself alone in the dark and ready to 'swoon almost with fear'.

ACT 3 SCENE 1

Lines 1–73: The artisans rehearse in the glade where Titania sleeps. Theatrical self-awareness is evident throughout the scene, particularly in the allocation of 'This green plot' as their stage and 'this hawthorn brake' as their 'tiring-house', as stage becomes woodland in the audience's imagination and is then transformed back into a stage in the minds of the characters. They discuss the details of staging, worrying about the lion or Pyramus' death upsetting the ladies in the audience, and considering how they will convey moonshine. Their simplistic approach once again emphasizes the sophistication of the wider performance.

Lines 74–200: Robin sustains the theatrical self-awareness as he observes the rehearsals and says that he will 'be an auditor, / An actor too perhaps'. Bottom makes a 'stage exit', followed by Robin. He returns with an ass's head as a result of Robin's spell and frightens the others away, pursued by Robin. Bottom, confused by their behaviour, decides that they mean to frighten him and sings so that they see that he is 'not afraid'. His singing wakes Titania, who, under the enchantment of the flower, is 'enamoured' and 'enthrallèd' of Bottom's singing and appearance and falls in love with him. She persuades him to remain in the woods with her, and calls upon four fairies to attend to him as she leads him to her bower.

ACT 3 SCENE 2

Lines 1–40: Oberon wonders what Titania now 'must dote on'. Robin appears and reports that she is in love with 'a monster', recounting the events of the previous scene. He says that he has put the juice in the Athenian's eyes, but as Demetrius and Hermia enter, it becomes clear that Oberon and Robin do not mean the same Athenian. They stand aside and watch.

Lines 41–121: Hermia believes that Demetrius has 'slain Lysander in his sleep', as there can be no other explanation for his leaving her. Demetrius denies this and realizes that there is no point in following Hermia, who leaves. He rests and falls asleep. Oberon realizes Robin's mistake and sends him to fetch Helena, then places the juice on Demetrius' eyelids while chanting a spell. Robin reports that Helena is on her way, followed by Lysander. He revels in the situation and suggests they enjoy the 'sport' of watching how 'two at once woo one'.

Lines 122–357: As Lysander tries to convince Helena that he loves her, Demetrius wakes up. Under the influence of the flower, he too falls in love with Helena, but she thinks that they are both mocking her. Hermia enters, having heard Lysander's voice, and demands to know why he left her. Lysander declares his love for Helena and his hatred of Hermia, who says that 'it cannot be'. Helena, however, thinks that Hermia is part of 'this confed'racy' and that all three are joined to spite her. She berates the bewildered Hermia, reminding her of their close friendship since childhood – 'Two lovely berries moulded on one stem' – and accuses her of encouraging Lysander and Demetrius.

Lysander challenges Demetrius to a duel. Hermia desperately tries to remind him of the love they share, but he insists that he hates her and loves Helena. Hermia turns on Helena, accusing her of stealing Lysander's love. The two women argue, insulting each other over their respective heights – Hermia describes Helena as a 'painted maypole' – but their repeated use of the words 'low' and 'lower' also apply to their positions in the esteem of the two men, again emphasizing the notion that it is the desire of others that creates worth. Demetrius and Lysander leave together to fight their duel and Helena and Hermia also exit.

Lines 358–408: Oberon suggests that Robin 'wilfully' caused the confusion, which he denies, saying that he did as Oberon requested, ''nointed an Athenian's eyes', although he does confess to finding sport in the resulting 'jangling'. Oberon commands Robin to 'overcast the night' and lead Lysander and Demetrius astray, so that they cannot meet and fight. He is to lead them around until they fall asleep, exhausted, and then put the juice of a different herb into Lysander's eyes, which will make all that has happened 'seem a dream'. While Robin does this, Oberon is going to beg Titania for the Indian boy and release her from the spell. Robin says that they must be quick as daylight is approaching – perhaps a metaphor for the impending restoration of order – and fairies 'themselves exile from light'. Oberon argues that he can exist in daylight, but agrees that a quick resolution is needed.

Lines 409–479: Pretending to be first Demetrius, then Lysander, Robin leads both characters around the wood, making sure that they never meet, until they are both so tired that they lie down and sleep. Helena and Hermia arrive separately and, not seeing the others, decide to sleep until daylight. Robin squeezes the herb's juice onto Lysander's eyelids so that he will love Hermia again, but Demetrius is left in love with Helena, so, as Robin says, 'all shall be well'.

ACT 4 SCENE 1

Lines 1–103: Titania dotes upon Bottom, caressing his 'fair large ears'. Bottom gives orders to Titania's attendants to scratch him, until he grows sleepy. Titania twists herself around him as 'doth the woodbine the sweet honeysuckle' and they sleep. Oberon, who has been watching them unseen, says to Robin that he begins to feel sorry for Titania, who has given him the changeling boy. He instructs Robin to change Bottom back so that he may return to Athens believing it all to have been 'the fierce vexation of a dream' and releases a confused Titania from the spell. Oberon and Titania dance, then leave as the morning approaches, emphasizing their place in the shadowy world, away from the light and the human order that it represents.

Lines 104–222: Theseus and his party stumble upon the sleeping lovers, and assume that, like them, they are all there to 'observe / The rite of May'. Remembering that Hermia must 'give answer of her choice', Theseus commands that the huntsmen wake them with their horns. Lysander admits to running away with Hermia and Egeus calls for 'the law, upon his head', saying that Lysander would have 'defeated' Demetrius of a wife. Demetrius, however, says that although he pursued them 'in fury', he now 'by some power' finds his 'love to Hermia, / Melted' and the only 'pleasure' of his 'eye' is Helena. Theseus says that they will hear more 'anon', but for now he overrules Egeus' will and decrees that Hermia shall marry Lysander and Demetrius shall marry Helena, sharing in the ceremony with himself and Hippolyta. The lovers discuss the dreamlike quality of events, but agree that they are now awake and must follow Theseus. Bottom wakes alone and confused, talking of the dream he has had. He leaves to get Quince to record his dream as a ballad.

ACT 4 SCENE 2

The other artisans look for Bottom, as the play is 'marred' without him. Snug reports that the marriages have taken place, and that if they could have performed before the duke (beneficiaries of preferment) they would have been 'made men'. Bottom appears and they set off for the palace.

ACT 5 SCENE 1

Lines 1–109: Theseus and Hippolyta discuss the lovers' stories, and Theseus comments on how 'The lunatic, the lover and the poet / Are of imagination all compact', thus highlighting the confused realities within the play, but also its metatheatrical element. They greet the lovers and discuss the possibility of some entertainment 'Between our after-supper and bedtime.' Egeus gives Theseus a list of possible 'sports' and he selects the artisans' play.

Lines 110–367: The play-within-the-play provides both linguistic and visual comedy and theatrical self-awareness is present in both the contrast with the wider performance and the presence of the two 'audiences'. Both comedy and self-awareness are heightened by the interjections of the onstage audience. The performance concludes and Theseus orders everyone to bed, as ''tis almost fairy time'.

Lines 368–435: The fairies return and their final verses, a blessing on the three couples' marriages, evoke their world and their place in mortal lives and imaginations. Robin's meta-theatrical epilogue to the audience suggests that if the play has offended, they think of it as 'a dream', a final confusion of reality and illusion in the audience's mind.

A MIDSUMMER NIGHT'S DREAM IN PERFORMANCE: THE RSC AND BEYOND

The best way to understand a Shakespeare play is to see it or ideally to participate in it. By examining a range of productions, we may gain a sense of the extraordinary variety of approaches and interpretations that are possible – a variety that gives Shakespeare his unique capacity to be reinvented and made 'our contemporary' four centuries after his death.

We begin with a brief overview of the play's theatrical and cinematic life, offering historical perspectives on how it has been performed. We then analyse in more detail a series of productions staged over the last half-century by the Royal Shakespeare Company. The sense of dialogue between productions that can only occur when a company is dedicated to the revival and investigation of the Shakespeare canon over a long period, together with the uniquely comprehensive archival resource of promptbooks, pro-gramme notes, reviews and interviews held on behalf of the RSC at the Shakespeare Birthplace Trust in Stratford-upon-Avon, allows an 'RSC stage history' to become a crucible in which the chemistry of the play can be explored.

Finally, we go to the horse's mouth. Modern theatre is dominated by the figure of the director. He, or sometimes she (like musical conducting, theatre directing remains a male-dominated profession), must hold together the whole play, whereas the actor must concentrate on his or her part. The director's viewpoint is therefore especially valuable. Shakespeare's plasticity is wonderfully revealed when we hear directors of highly successful productions answering the same questions in very different ways.

FOUR CENTURIES OF THE *DREAM*: AN OVERVIEW

Interpretations and ideas about the play have altered radically over the four centuries since its first performance around 1595–96. Theories suggesting that it was written to celebrate an aristocratic wedding have fallen into disfavour. The Quarto edition of 1600 claims that it had 'beene sundry times publickly acted' by the Lord Chamberlain's Men (later the King's Men) and it may be the play referred to in a letter which records a court performance of the 'play of Robin goode-fellow' on 1 January 1604.[1] There is no further evidence of performance before the Restoration of the monarchy in 1660. Will Kempe, the company's chief comic actor at this period, may originally have played Bottom and Richard Burbage Oberon, possibly doubling the role with Theseus. The text suggests Titania's fairies were small-sized and may have been played by boys, although recent research based on the pattern of appearances of fairies and mechanicals suggests that the same actors may well have doubled these parts,[2] a theory perhaps corroborated by the cast list of the 1661 droll, *The Merry conceited Humours of Bottome the Weaver*, which suggests that Snout, Snug and Starveling as Wall, Lion and Moonshine 'likewise may present three Faries'.[3]

The play's combination of realism and fantasy was not to the taste of Restoration audiences. Samuel Pepys judged it 'the most insipid ridiculous play that I ever saw in my life'.[4] Eighteenth- and nineteenth-century taste preferred romanticized, sanitized versions of Shakespeare's plays. The drama was heavily influenced by French neo-classicism's strict adherence to the unities of time, place and action: decorum was observed and bawdy language eliminated. Theatrical productions emphasized spectacle and there were a number of operatic adaptations which featured the play's courtly aspects, with music and dancing. William Hazlitt, writing in 1817, argued against all performance on the grounds that theatrical representation is, by its very nature, gross and material, unlike Shakespeare's airy conception: 'The *Midsummer Night's Dream*, when acted, is converted from a delightful fiction into a dull pantomime. All that is finest in the play is lost in the representation.

The spectacle was grand; but the spirit was evaporated, the genius was fled. Poetry and the stage do not agree well together.'[5] In fact the version that Hazlitt saw was most likely Frederick Reynolds' 1816 adaptation, as much a musical as a play.

From the Restoration onwards, thanks to technical innovation, increasingly sophisticated theatrical machinery and movable stage sets, spectacular operatic versions of the play predominated, culminating in the extravaganzas of the great Georgian and Victorian actor-managers such as John Philip Kemble, Charles Kean, Henry Irving and Beerbohm Tree. Ballet-style productions featured choruses of fairies, processions with spears and trumpets, and acres of gauze. Mid- and late-nineteenth-century productions focused on pictorial realism and attempted to 'illustrate' the plays. Great emphasis was placed on the recreation of historical accuracy in costume and sets to create a complete theatrical illusion. For example, James Grieve, the designer for Kean's 1858 production, aimed at historical accuracy – the playbill boasted that 'The Acropolis, on its rocky eminence, surrounded by marble Temples, has been restored, together with the Theatre of Bacchus, wherein multitudes once thronged to listen to the majestic poetry of Aeschylus, Sophocles, and Euripides.'[6] Realism was taken to the extreme, reproducing Quince's workshop and stage properties supposedly made by him, which used descriptions of objects found in the excavations of Pompeii and Herculaneum for the tools. Beerbohm Tree's production actually recreated the 'bank where the wild thyme blows' and imported live rabbits to scamper across it in his 1911 revival.[7]

Adaptations of *A Midsummer Night's Dream* separated out the different elements of the play. The anonymous droll published in 1661 under the title *Bottom the Weaver* was chiefly concerned with the 'rude mechanicals', though it provided abbreviated roles for Oberon, Titania and Robin. 'Duke', 'Duchess' and two 'Lords' represented the courtly audience. In 1692 Thomas Betterton produced *The Fairy Queen, An Opera* with music by Henry Purcell. This included court characters, 'The Fairies', 'The Comedians', and a masque at the end of each act, including 'Juno', 'Chinese Men and

Women', 'A Chorus of Chineses' (*sic*), 'A Dance of 6 Monkeys', 'An Entry of a Chinese Man and Woman', 'A Grand Dance of 24 Chineses'. Richard Leveridge's *The Comick Masque of Pyramus and Thisbe* (1716) contained the mechanicals plus 'Mr Semibreve the Composer', 'Crochet', 'Gamut', as well as 'Prologue', 'Pyramus', 'Wall', 'Lyon', 'Moon-shine', 'Thisbe' and 'Epilogue'. And the 1763 adaptation *A Fairy Tale in Two Acts* featured 'Men' (the mechanicals) and 'Fairies'.

In 1775 David Garrick staged *The Fairies: An Opera taken from A Midsummer Night's Dream* which featured courtiers and fairies but no mechanicals. It included twenty-eight songs and was moderately successful, certainly in comparison with his later five-act, thirty-three song version – that lasted only one performance. In 1816 Frederick Reynolds presented his version of *A Midsummer Night's Dream*. The title page describes it as 'Written by Shakespeare: with Alterations, Additions, and New Songs; as it is performed at the Theatre-Royal, Covent-Garden'. In his 'Advertisement' for the play, Reynolds denigrated Garrick's earlier version. Nevertheless, he used quite a lot of the material from it, notably the songs, and his text was almost as abbreviated, although he did reinstate the mechanicals. Lucia Elizabeth Vestris' 1840 production, in which she played Oberon, although still lavish and incorporating elements of opera and ballet, restored much of Shakespeare's text. Felix Mendelssohn had originally written the overture to his 'Incidental Music to *A Midsummer Night's Dream*' in 1826 (opus 21), composing the rest of the score sixteen years later (opus 61) for Ludwig Tieck's 1843 revival at the Potsdam Court Theatre.

In 1853 Samuel Phelps staged a highly successful production at Sadler's Wells, in which he played Bottom. Three years later, Charles Kean's revival at the Princess' was equally successful – the nine-year-old Ellen Terry played Robin, an experience recalled in her autobiography.[8] Augustin Daly's three American productions (1873, 1888, 1895–96) were lavish and spectacularly staged, with a ballet of fifty children in Act 3. Beerbohm Tree's productions were even more extravagant, but no less popular with audiences and critics alike: 'No scene has ever been put upon the stage more beautiful than the wood near Athens in which the fairies revel and the lovers play their game of hide-and-seek.'[9]

1. Victorian staging with elaborate set and huge troupe of gossamer-clad fairies.

The self-reflexive quality of Shakespearean drama was eliminated in all these adaptations and the conventions of Elizabethan staging regarded as limitations to be overcome. The end of the Victorian period saw the beginnings of a contemporary reaction against theatrical realism and the spectacular in favour of simpler, faster-paced productions which used all or most of Shakespeare's text on recreated Elizabethan-style stages. The most influential directors in this move were William Poel and Harley Granville-Barker. Gordon Craig also offered simplified staging of the play and a full text. Barker's production of *A Midsummer Night's Dream* at the Savoy Theatre in 1914 created a critical sensation which was not wholly favourable. In his *Preface* to *A Midsummer Night's Dream*, Barker argued that the non-realism of the play, like the 'greatness' of *King Lear* and the 'scope of the action' of *Antony and Cleopatra*, were problematic for the scenic productions of the modern theatre. He suggested producing the play on Shakespeare's own terms, with an appeal to the ear and the imagination of the audience. The structure of the play should be kept flexible. He also advocated the use of folk music and dances as opposed to the, by then customary, Mendelssohn score. Barker made it clear, though, that his emphasis was Shakespeare's own theme:

> In fine, Shakespeare has a theme, which only poetry can fully illuminate, and he trusts to poetry. Nor will he risk any conflict of interest, all the rest of his dramatist's equipment must cry small for the occasion. Wherefore we in our turn must plan the play's interpretation upon these terms. Poetry, poetry; everything to serve and nothing to compete with it![10]

Barker's production did not meet with universal approbation. Nevertheless, it was revolutionary for its time and set in train the fashion for stylized and non-naturalistic productions. His ideas were influenced by a modernist aesthetic which rejected realism and romanticism.

This aesthetic development found perhaps its most complete expression in Peter Brook's 1970 RSC production (discussed in detail below). In 1992, the French Canadian director, Robert Lepage, also offered a dark reading of the play for Britain's National Theatre, emphasizing its psychological and sexual elements. While incorporating certain aspects of Brook's version, such as the acrobatics, in other regards Lepage reacted against it. Most dramatically, Brook's celebrated white box was replaced by a mud pool. Critics at the time seem to have been confounded by this, but the hints are there in many film versions from Max Reinhardt onwards which feature water, mud and pools, culminating in the mud-wrestling in Michael Hoffman's 1999 version. Hoffman, however, was probably inspired in turn by Lepage, which suggests something of the circularity of cross-media cultural influences today.

The play's spectacular potential has recommended it to operatic composers from Purcell to Benjamin Britten and Michael Tippett via Mendelssohn. Tippett's *The Midsummer Marriage* (1946–52) was inspired by Shakespeare's play. It contains a similar combination of ordinary mortals and supernatural elements. The mortals are two pairs of lovers on the brink of marriage. The supernatural element features a temple with a priest and priestess. Benjamin Britten's *A Midsummer Night's Dream* (1960) evokes the wood, where his opera starts with discordant glissandos on the cello and a chorus of boys as fairies. Specific instruments are imagined for different groups of characters throughout, in a witty musical way. Fairies are strings, wind section and percussion, especially the xylophone for Robin. The mechanicals are characterized by the brass section, the trombone for Bottom and, not surprisingly, the flute for Flute. The most striking characterization is the counter-tenor part for Oberon, which creates an eerie otherworldly effect. Titania sings a beautiful, lyrical aria to Bottom as an ass, and the encounter of Pyramus and Thisbe is written as a subtle parody of Puccini.

The combination of Shakespeare's play and Mendelssohn's music has proved inspirational to choreographers from Petipa (1877), to George Balanchine (1962) and Frederick Ashton's *The Dream* (1964). Balanchine created *A Midsummer Night's Dream* for the New York City Ballet. He was inspired principally by Mendelssohn's music and, in order to produce his first full-length ballet in America, added extra music from other works of Mendelssohn's. Ashton's *The Dream* is also set in the wood and focuses on the fairies and the lovers. Of the mechanicals only Bottom features as a rustic transformed by Robin who wakes Titania. Lindsay Kemp, who played Robin in a 1994 *A Midsummer Night's Dream* directed by Celestino Coronado, effectively turned the play into 'Puck's Dream', in which the action opens and closes with him asleep wrapped in a cobweb. The production was clearly related to Reinhardt's influential 1935 film, on the one hand, and Peter Brook's staging, influenced by the Polish critic Jan Kott (see below), on the other.

The play's mix of comedy, romance and magic has proved irresistible to filmmakers, starting with a twelve-minute American silent version in 1909 directed by J. Stuart Blackton and Charles Kent for the Vitagraph Company of America. This is a radically simplified version of the story, shot outdoors on a windy day. There is an obvious attempt at authentic Athenian costume and presumably equally authentic fairy costume. Fairies seem to be female. Robin is a little girl and there are two other little girl fairies. Oberon has turned inexplicably into Penelope.

Max Reinhardt's 1935 film won well-deserved Oscars for Ralph Dawson, Best Film Editing, and Hal Mohr, Best Cinematography. Mohr was never nominated but was the one and only person to win due to a popular write-in campaign. The following year the Academy changed the rules so that it couldn't happen again. The scenes in the wood with a chorus of fairies and an orchestra of elves and gnomes are brilliantly shot and directed to Mendelssohn's music, arranged by Erich Korngold. The overall effect is exhilarating and the casting full of surprises, including a very young Mickey Rooney as Robin and James Cagney as Bottom.

Peter Hall's 1968 film, a version of his RSC stage production, shot at Compton Verney (less than ten miles from Stratford), betrays its age in the women's costumes – Hippolyta, Hermia and Helena are wearing 1960s miniskirts with long boots. The fairies are flower children and Judi Dench wears nothing except a body stocking and some strategically placed flowers. The 1992 *Shakespeare: The Animated Tales: A Midsummer Night's Dream*, abridged by Leon Garfield, is one of the most successful of this Russian/British collaboration in which a dozen of the most popular plays were reworked for children. Drawing and animation are excellent – incorporating expressive touches such as Titania's lips turning from green to red when she's 'enamoured of an ass'.

Michael Hoffman's 1999 film is a lush romantic version in which the emphasis is on love and sex. Set in nineteenth-century Italy, the opening titles announce that 'necklines were high and parents were rigid', 'bustles were in decline' and that 'newfangled invention, the bicycle' was on the rise. The central performance is Kevin Kline's romantic Bottom.

The RSC, in conjunction with Film4, produced a screen version (1996) based on Adrian Noble's 1994 stage production. It reveals its debt to Peter Brook in the modernist set and bright, modern clothes. The story is mediated through the experience of a little boy. The opening shot pans around the child's bedroom and finally focuses on him asleep. In answer to the question 'Whose dream is it?', the answer becomes 'a child's' – a problematic device in many respects.

Modern critical and theatrical practice responds to the play's meta-theatricality, to its knowing self-awareness of life as inherently performative in a way that speaks to post-modern theories relating to the loss of the real and the superabundance of simulacra. Performance styles have moved away from representations of pictorial realism to engage the audience directly. Noble's and Elijah Moshinsky's 1981 BBC television production both have Robin employ the 'forbidden look': a stare straight to camera, analogous to the actor's direct address to the audience in Shakespeare's own theatre. Contemporary theatre has knocked down the fourth wall and is concerned to play with knowing irony on the relationship between actor, role and audience. *A Midsummer Night's Dream* resonates with our cultural self-reflexivity: modernity, or rather post-modernity, responds to the play's ironic confusion of planes of reality and blurring of boundaries between the political, emotional, psychological, sexual and spiritual. At one level the play suggests that life is complex and problematic, but things will work out. But at the margins, contained within the play's various fictions, it recognizes only too clearly that they may not.

AT THE RSC

The Shifting Point

> In *A Midsummer Night's Dream* the war amongst the fairies has resulted not only in a loss of control of elements and seasons: human beings also have become at odds with each other. It is a kind of cold war and all life as well as all nature has been set a-jangling. It seems that the mortals can find peace only when Oberon and Titania have found it. And more than this – they can find it only after being drawn into the world of Dreams back to the roots of mythology and folklore and into Oberon's domain of half-light – more revealing by far in its fantasies than the world of Reality.
>
> (Programme note from *A Midsummer Night's Dream*, 1960, Old Vic, directed by Michael Langham)

To the Elizabethans, seasonal festivals and significant calendar events like May Day, Midsummer and Twelfth Night, were not just important landmarks framing the cycle of the year, but in their celebration acted as a release valve for human behaviour. The energy normally occupied in maintaining inhibition was freed for celebration. These times of misrule when social norms were turned on their head had a cathartic power, and for the young they often involved 'a right of passage between generations, a means of making the transition from the old world to the new'.[11] The sanctioned freeing from society's usual constraints was seen as a release, but also, by contrast, as an affirmation of the rules and morals that normally guided people's lives.

The psychological benefits of the May Day festival became key to most post-1960 productions of *A Midsummer Night's Dream*. The exploration of the relationship between the conscious and the unconscious, of the real world and the fairy world, turned the court of Theseus into the embodiment of society's repression and the forest of Athens into a therapeutic playground for an exploration of the self.

After Jan Kott's essay 'Titania and the Ass's Head' (in his *Shakespeare our Contemporary*, published in English translation in 1964), productions of the *Dream* picked up on the strand of dark sexuality evident in the text. Peter Brook, whose landmark production of 1970 marked a shifting point in how directors thought about the play, pointed out that 'The *Dream* is not a piece for the kids – it's a very powerful sexual play.'[12] He also commented:

> The *Dream* is a play about magic, spirits, fairies. Today we don't believe in any one of those things and yet, perhaps, we do. The fairy imagery which the Victorian and even post-Victorian tradition has given us in relation to the *Dream* has to be rejected – it has died on us. But one can't take an anti-magical, and down-to-earth view of the *Dream* . . . the interest in working on the *Dream* is to take a play which is apparently composed of very artificial, unreal elements and to discover that it is a true, a real play.[13]

Rejecting the 'cute, gauzy, bewinged creatures'[14] of the Victorian era, modern productions reinterpreted how magic was represented in the play with a variety of tricks used by weird and wonderful fairies. Attention to the whole art of theatrical illusion, in the staging, and in the Pyramus and Thisbe scene, also emphasized the

2. Production of 1959, with a suggestion of Queen Elizabeth. The kind of gentle, picturesque Dream that was reacted against in an influential essay by the Polish critic Jan Kott, which proposed a darker and far more sexually charged, even brutal, reading of the play.

meta-theatrical nature of the play, to a degree that had only been glanced at by productions of the early twentieth century.

Peter Brook's 1970 production was almost without question the most influential single production of any Shakespeare play in the second half of the twentieth century. In the words of the critic Trevor R. Griffiths,

> Other directors of *A Midsummer Night's Dream* had already seen the need to remove various sentimental accretions, others had made the fairies a strong physical presence in the lovers' quarrels, others had seen possibilities in doubling the mortal and fairy rulers or stressing the therapeutic value of the events in the wood ... but [Brook's] triumph lay in creating a powerful crystallisation of these various elements into a unified and cohesive whole.[15]

No director could avoid the influence of this staging of the *Dream*: 'If they did not turn their backs on Brook's achievement, [they] tried somehow to get around it or to find other ways of presenting the play without going to such extremes as Brook felt compelled to do. Or they reverted to something closer to traditional "picture-book" versions of the play.'[16]

Exploring Brook's production and those that followed, this section will examine how the treatment of *A Midsummer Night's Dream* reflects a change in critical thinking about the play. Looking at abstract stagings, nightmarish dreams, and the more overtly sexual take on the scenes in the forest, we will see how the play has come into its own in the latter part of the twentieth century, exploring issues which previous stagings of Shakespeare's magical play had neglected.

'All that We See or Seem / Is but a Dream within a Dream'[17]

In 1970, the theatre critic J. C. Trewin remarked that 'We have met the fantasy in so many forms; over-decorated and under-decorated, as a swooningly Victorian album or as a Jacobean masque. The

3. Peter Brook's 1970 production, with white box and trapeze.

Wood has been a complicated forest and austere, moon-silvered thicket, or a garden in Regent's Park.'[18] With productions of the *Dream* occurring every three or four years in the RSC's repertoire, the difficulty for any director is to find new and interesting settings that will emphasize and add to the play's meaning rather than just decorate it. There is also the dilemma of trying to show a correlation between and a melding of the mortal and fairy worlds.

The traditional wooded glade was already beginning to fade from twentieth-century visions of the *Dream* when Peter Brook blew away all previous conceptions, conventions and cliches with a radically different staging concept. What he called his 'celebration of theatre' put emphasis on the artificiality of the medium, and demonstrated the impossibility of designing a representational world for the play that a modern audience would believe in. The stage became a blank sheet on which the actors made their own magic through the art of theatre itself. Brook's designer, Sally Jacobs, recalled:

> Peter wanted to investigate all the ideas of the play, such as the variations on the theme of love, with a group of actors – always inter-relating so that they could play each other's parts – in a very small, very intimate acting area. So the story would remain clear. It wouldn't be blown up into a big production number, with fogs, forests, and Athens, and all of that pretence. We would just keep it very, very simple and make it a presentation of actors performing a play. In doing 'The Dream' that way, we could let it be surprising, inconsistent, the source material always being the text rather than a 'scheme'.[19]

Jacobs designed a three-sided white box set, which was held in a constant white light so no trick could go unmissed. Darkness was removed from the forest and the action and characters thrown into sharp relief. The play opened without the traditional safety curtain (something we are used to now, but which was out of the ordinary at the time), with the full company juggling and tumbling. The set was seen variously by reviewers as a child's play box, 'a squash court, a clinic, a scientific research station, an operating theatre, a gymnasium and a big top ... Two doors were cut in the back wall, two slits in the sides, two ladders set at the downstage edges, and a gallery or catwalk round its top [allowing] the musicians and fairies to gaze down at the players.'[20] The symmetry of the set with the doubling of the characters emphasized Hermia's words when she comes out of the 'dream', 'everything seems double'. It also created an intense and intimate space where the tension never let up.

Brook's device for distinguishing the different worlds was simple. There was no change in setting; the characters wore long robes in the Athenian court which they quickly removed to reveal their fairy-world costumes, like circus performers readying themselves for action. On leaving the forest at the end of the play the actors simply put the robes back on. Brook was keen to stress that the fairies, the aristocrats and the mechanicals did not occupy different worlds but were facets of the same world. 'The more one examines the play, the more one sees how these worlds interweave', he said.[21] Irving Wardle, reviewing the production, commented:

> It provides an environment for the *Dream* which removes the sense of being earthbound: it is natural here for characters to fly ... Brook's company give the play a continuously animated physical line, occupying the whole cubic space of the stage and they ship up and down ladders and stamp about in enormous stilts ... We are accustomed to seeing them as inhabitants of different worlds. Brook shows them as members of the same world. Egeus's loss of his daughter is matched by Oberon's loss of his Indian boy. 'This same progeny of evils comes from our debate', says Titania; and as Sara Kestelman delivers it, reclining on the huge scarlet ostrich feather that serves as her bower, the line is meant to embrace the whole action.[22]

The acrobatics, circus skills and trapeze acts of the actors defined them as magical beings that could defy gravity. In keeping with this, the costumes of the fairies resembled a cross between Chinese acrobats and romper-suits. Oberon, Titania and Robin wore vivid primary colours, whereas the fairies of the lower hierarchy wore grey silk:

The fairies were no longer thought of as decorative, but as functional. They appeared as hefty circus hands when they swept up the confetti, as familiar spirits when they physically controlled the movements of the lovers and demoniacally trapped them in their steel forest, and as amoral trolls when they stripped Snug of his trousers and created an obscene phallus for Bottom.[23]

The box set that Adrian Noble opted for in 1994 was reminiscent of Brook's, but in its simplicity created an environment which suited his particular vision of the play: a low-walled, single-doored chamber was dominated by a trapeze, suggesting the surreal strangeness of a dream. Noble remarked that 'of course in its first performance the *Dream* would not have had a wood. What we want to achieve is a sort of fluidity whereby the action is not held up by endless clumsy scene changes.'[24] The bare set allowed the fluidity of action, but also, 'never let the audience forget that we are in the midst of a dream. At certain points in the evening, we hear the sound of heavy breathing, as if we were eavesdropping on the sleeping Shakespeare as he conjures his own play.'[25]

Designer Anthony Ward, on discussing the concept with Noble, recalled that

we found ourselves talking in terms of abstract design, which led me to think immediately of the work of the ... [Belgian] Surrealist painter René Magritte ... we were inspired by the idea of *A Midsummer Night's Dream* as a study of the world of dreaming and sleep. So what we needed was a design style which would allow us to present the conscious, real, world overlapping with the world of the sub-conscious ... [Magritte's] paintings juxtapose items from the ordinary, real world in a way which makes them seem strange and gives them a new and interesting resonance. So, in our production you see ordinary, household objects, such as an umbrella, transformed to serve a completely different function.[26]

Umbrellas were used as a mean of levitation and flight. 'Titania's chief mode of conveyance – and bedroom – [was] a vast, suspended

Magritte umbrella sumptuously lined with red quilt.'[27] The use of doors which popped up through the floor and aided the action of the lovers had a psychological significance: 'Why the doors and all the rushing in and out of them that duly ensues? You hardly need ask. People are passing from waking to dreaming, consciousness to sub-consciousness, ignorance and self-discovery.'[28]

In order to differentiate between the Athenian court and the forest, Noble's lighting designer, Chris Parry, lit the bare set with colours that were descriptive rather than representational – scarlet for Athens and indigo for the enchanted wood:

> [Noble] didn't want trees, a forest, or anything like that … I wanted to achieve a forest made out of beams of light and light bulbs … most of the action … takes place at night, but rather than using the straight-forwards 'night-time' blue I have used a lot of purples and lavenders … very sensuous colours which suggest the mysterious magical quality of night.[29]

Abstract stagings of the *Dream* are often met with slight hostility by audiences who come to the theatre with a preconceived idea of what the play should look like. There is still a tendency for people to hark back to the Victorian image of the fairy in its idyllic forest setting. This holds a certain nostalgia, an innocence, going back to a time in history when people were still willing to believe in such things. However, the image is still prevalent in the social consciousness, and one that can still be found in most gift and card shops. Where these productions have succeeded is in the creation of a completely new magical space with a physical theatricality to complement Shakespeare's text.

'To Wake and be Free / From this Nightmare We Writhe In'[30]

Brook's production revealed to many viewers and critics that 'the *Dream* is a fearful play'.[31] Picking up on this dark strand, many productions since have emphasised the nightmarish elements evident in the text. No more so than the RSC's 2002 production, which made direct references to modern horror films. The *Guardian*'s veteran critic Michael Billington observed that

> Richard Jones provides something closer to a gothic nightmare ... designer Giles Cadle [does] everything possible to create 'the fierce vexation of a dream' ... Shakespeare's Athenian wood, here dominated by a humanised tree with claw-like branches, becomes a sinister conflation of *Friday The Thirteenth*, *Hallowe'en* and *Edward Scissorhands*. Fast breeding flies swarm over Cadle's box set, hands emerge through the walls as in Polanski's *Repulsion* and the transformed Bottom sports a disfigured mask with phallic ears while Puck carries his original head tucked underneath his arm.[32]

The disorientating and starkly black and white set, like an 'optical magician's *camera obscura*',[33] combined the surreal and the abstract: 'a wonky oblong that's half-moon, half-egg; cigarette-like cylinders with steps cut into their ends; a sort of squashed ice-cream cone that weirdly doubles as a train on which the rude mechanicals, themselves a grey-garbed ... blend of Soviet convicts and British hikers, decide to arrive'.[34]

The sex and horror that Jan Kott found in the play were taken to their extreme: 'Titania resembling a debauched Hamburg nightclub queen'[35] and Robin taking Hermia's line 'O hell! To choose love by another's eyes' literally, by physically removing and then swapping the eyes of the lovers. Many reviewers felt the actors and the plot were overwhelmed by the mechanics of this imaginative design. They describe them as 'competing' with the set and the interpretation of the play, which often worked against the text. However, others felt that this production tapped 'into something important. In giving us the Bard as Goth, and putting the "witch" back into bewitching, it reminds us how dark and disturbing this play – Shakespeare's most beguiling – can be.'[36]

Albeit with a subtler tone, this emphasis was also strong in John Barton's 1981 production. He, too, in the words of critic Jay Halio,

> totally rejected any cute, gauzy, bewinged creatures and opted instead for wooden puppets that closely resembled the kind of

Victorian dolls beloved by the makers of horror films ...
Manipulated by black clad actors and actresses who also spoke
their lines, those fairies Shakespeare failed to nominate were
dubbed in the programme 'Black Boy', 'Girl with Red Hair',
'Broken Head', etc. ... At one point, Oberon had to fight his way
past a mass of screeching dolls to get to Titania's bower.[37]

These puppet fairies first appeared, flying out from a wicker prop
basket, trailing coloured streamers in various stages of disintegration
and decay that moved 'in large sweeping and diving motions
[against a] black cyclorama, they seem like small macabre souls,
darting silently in the blackness ... They hover in the air
protectively, around Titania, and they watch anxiously as the fairy
king and queen quarrel, shifting and darting, their puppet limbs
sometimes clacking quietly in the silence like bones.'[38] The style of
the whole production led reviewers to question what had been
described as the RSC's salute to the royal wedding of Prince Charles
and Diana Spencer. 'If so,' wrote Benedict Nightingale in the *New
Statesman*,

it's an ambiguous one, with something akin to two fingers
sprouting from the patriotically outstretched arm ... the
doubling of real and fairy king and queen, with the suggestion
that Oberon's revenge on Titania reflects and resolves Theseus's
subconscious hostilities towards Hippolyta, his bride-to-be. In
other words, Chuck might feel better about Di if he imagined her
having sex with a prole with a donkey's head.[39]

In Gregory Doran's entertaining 2005 production the mortal world
was 'a chilly, soulless place, with a suggestion of the totalitarian
state about it'.[40] More nightmarish and unforgiving than the fairy
world, Theseus's military uniform made him resemble 'a fascist
leader'.[41] With a death threat hanging over her head, Hermia's
escape into the forest with Lysander takes her from the proverbial
frying pan into the fire. Jonathan Slinger's refreshingly lugubrious
and mischievous Robin plays with the lovers as if they are puppets
for his amusement. In the hands of this curmudgeonly sceptic, who

has no qualms about his treatment of mortals, one would fear for their fate if he were not tempered by his master, Oberon, who feels for the lovers' plight.

The *Spectator*'s reviewer, Patrick Carnegy, remarked that

> The fairy band is a motley crew of ragamuffins who have one important accomplishment – their magic is that of puppeteers ... Doran gives us the changeling boy as an exquisitely animated puppet ... Bottom's attendants materialise as a macabre collection of doll-puppets manipulated by their fairy alter egos ... whenever Mustardseed opens his mouth to speak, his head pops up and away off his body.[42]

The themes of manipulation and entrapment in the forest scenes culminated when Robin led the lovers 'Up and down, up and down'. Working together, the fairies physically manipulated the lovers' movements like their 'doll-puppets', holding on to their limbs and guiding them to the appointed place for Robin to send them to sleep.

Nightmares, as other dreams, offer the possibility for self-exploration and understanding. The lovers, Titania and Bottom all learn through a period of transformation, akin to a waking dream, that the exploration of the worst parts of themselves can free them from nightmare. Scholar Stanley Wells commented in the pro-gramme note that

> As the lovers go off to marriage, we are likely to feel that they have been through a necessary but profoundly disturbing experience, and that now they are safely on the other side of it. The experience has grown 'to something of great constancy', enriching their lives just as Bottom's 'rare vision' enriches his. They bring back into the ordinary world something that they learned in the world of imagination. The illusory has its part in the total experience of reality.[43]

In avoiding the baggage of treating the *Dream* as a light fairy-piece for children many directors have chosen to focus on the darker elements of the play, with varying success. The difficulty for them arises in trying to strike a balance between the comedy and the darkness.

Everything seems Double

The doubling of the fairy and mortal characters in *A Midsummer Night's Dream* may appear now as the normal directorial choice. However, this development in staging has only been prevalent in the last fifty years. Through this device directors have explored the relationship between the mortals and the fairies in terms of the conscious and the unconscious.

In 1970 this was a relatively new innovation which radically altered the reading of the play, and extended the psychological journey of Bottom and the four lovers to all the mortals. Brook's *Dream* depicted the unconscious enactment of unresolved tensions which needed to be explored before the royal couple could come together in happy marriage at the end of the play. The director himself explained:

The play unfolds like a dream before [Theseus and Hippolyta's] wedding in which an almost identical couple appear – Oberon and Titania. Yet this other couple are in an opposition so great that, as Titania announces in a language of great strength, it brings about a complete schism in the natural order ... Thus on the one hand we have a man and woman in total dispute and, on the other, a man and woman coming together through a concord found out of a discord. The couples are so closely related that we felt that Oberon and Titania could easily be sitting inside the minds of Theseus and Hippolyta.[44]

In Bill Alexander's 1986 production only Hippolyta and Titania were doubled, while Theseus and Oberon were played by separate actors:

The key to Mr Alexander's interpretation lies in the moment when, as the rude mechanicals come on stage to rehearse, Janet McTeer's elegant, disdainful Hippolyta passes them on her way off. She and Bottom exchange a long appraising look across a social chasm. What follows is, in effect, Hippolyta's dream.[45]

This Hippolyta, described as 'glacial and contemptuous'[46] in the Athenian scenes, obviously did not relish the prospect of marriage to the boring Theseus. She 'has the opportunity to express an inner life – a slinkily clad ice-maiden whose fantasies are realized by transformation into a fairy queen of bewitchingly tender sexual desire'.[47] Her Oberon (Gerard Murphy) became the ideal partner, equal to her in physical strength and passion. The wordless coda at the start of the play also put a different spin on Titania's relationship with Bottom:

> In the wood, the affection between [Bottom] and [Titania] is played almost completely 'straight', emphasizing both its realness and its impossibility. Love that crosses barriers in the night's most hopeless 'dream', sprinkling regret over the ubiquitous frolics.[48]

> This Bottom was gentler and more sympathetic, a true alternative to the chauvinism of Theseus and Oberon; consequently, he drew from Titania a warm and tender response, which, if it did not entirely eliminate the element of lustful sensuality, de-emphasised it considerably.[49]

At the end of the play, Hippolyta stepped into the fairy ring and – as Titania – sang the blessing with Oberon to the newlyweds, harmonizing the worlds of the play, and emphasizing the connection between reality and dreams.

In Michael Boyd's 1999 production, the fairies were played as doppelgängers of the mortals, releasing their inner selves from their daytime personae. According to *Times* critic Benedict Nightingale,

> Theseus and Hippolyta become their subconscious selves, Oberon and Titania. They dream out their conflicts and marry happily. But Boyd takes the approach further … Athens itself sheds its superego and lets its id rampage, until Theseus, Hippolyta, lovers, mechanicals, everyone, are clattering together in a dance that Zorba himself would have found too anarchic.[50]

Aidan McArdle, who doubled as Robin and Philostrate, explains that Act 3 scene 2, in which Oberon comforts Robin's fear at the coming dawn, was given an added significance by the whole concept of the production:

> We had it in our heads as we played this ... that they were afraid of turning back into their daylight selves. As it gets light Puck must be transformed into that monster Philostrate – and Philostrate is as much a monster for Puck as Puck is for Philostrate.[51]

The opening scenes in the Athenian court contained virtually no colour; the characters were wrapped up in large dark overcoats. The fairy world emerged from the mortal world via a simple device:

> The repressed, regimented, grey court, reminiscent of Cold-War Russia, would move to the forest by way of the transformation scene, which would begin with artificial flowers (the first colour in the play) sprouting through the stage floor.[52]

The transformation from Athens to fairyland was enacted by two characters from the Athenian court who stripped off each other's clothes to reveal the 'fairy' beneath. This also signalled how the sexual war, and sexual frustrations of the fairy world, were impinging on the real world:

> Sirine Saba, Philostrate's side-kick in the court scenes, came on in her white gloves, fur hat, and spectacles. Philostrate appeared in the doorway behind her as she bent down – ostensibly to pick a flower, but somehow in a rather suggestive manner. Philostrate would then stalk her down the stage ... he would catch her up and ... be right behind her the next time she bent down. Philostrate had had an idiosyncratic little gesture, in the court scene, of stepping forward and rocking on his heels. This movement behind a girl bending down was, obviously, very sexual ... She would then turn, and slap me across the face. I would ... then remove her hat, pull off its ear-flaps and throw it away. She would ... then remove my glasses and break the arms

off ... take off my bowler hat, spit in it, and throw them all into the wings. Things would then escalate ... until we would be ripping the clothes off each other with frenzied energy. This was followed by energetic kissing, the fierceness of the love/hate relationship descending rapidly into pure sexuality. She would then run away in a very coy, teasing manner, which was the cue for the first line of the scene: 'How now, spirit, whither wander you?' ... the scene became directly about desire and passion – everything they had both been repressing at court.[53]

If We Shadows have Offended

Puritan writers such as Philip Stubbes were shocked by the degree of sexual licence taken at May Day and Midsummer Night festivals. His work *Anatomy of Abuses* published in 1583, then reprinted in 1585 and 1595 (very probably the same year in which Shakespeare wrote the *Dream*), spoke out against the pagan rituals still abundant in England at the time:

> All the young men and maids, old men and wives, run gadding over night to the woods, groves, hills, woods, and mountains, where they spend all the night in pleasant pastimes ... I have heard it credibly reported (and that *viva voce*) by men of great gravity and reputation, that of forty, three-score, or a hundred maids going to the wood over night, there have scarcely the third part of them returned home again undefiled. These be the fruits which these cursed pastimes bring forth.[54]

In 1642 the puritans closed the theatres. In 1644 the May festival was banned. From their representation in his plays, we can imagine that these were not Shakespeare's favourite people.

Most modern productions have the lovers go through various states of undress as they make their journey through the hostile forest. However, it is a mistake to think of this as just a sexual undressing. As the programme to Sheila Hancock's 1984 touring production suggested, it is also a process of self-discovery:

In sleep we have a reversion to a more primitive type of experience ... The dream becomes a revelation. It strips the ego of its artificial wrappings and exposes it in its native nudity. It brings up from the dim depths of our sub-conscious life the primal, instinctive impulses, and discloses to us a side of ourselves which connects us with the great sentient world.[55]

In a world where magic and the supernatural are no longer a part of everyday life, 'once we are out of childhood the closest we come to magic is through our dreams; in this extra-terrestrial world we meet the part of ourselves which we bury under social convention'.[56] In modern productions of *A Midsummer Night's Dream* that buried part of the self has invariably been depicted as the sexual self – in keeping with the aspect of the May, which so appalled Stubbes in Shakespeare's day. Shakespeare critic Mary Maher explains:

If the visual image of *A Midsummer Night's Dream* in the nineteenth century was the gauzy-winged fairy, the immediate icon of the late twentieth century was the up-thrust arm between Bottom's legs, the oversized ass's penis created by two actors positioned to show arousal in Peter Brook's 1970 staging of the play ... What Brook did was corrective; he was reinserting and reissuing the seminal strand of sexuality into the mainstream of the play's production history.[57]

Despite being in a recognizable tradition of modern productions of the *Dream*, Michael Boyd's 1999 production was criticized for its overtly sexual reading of the play. He warned the public before it opened:

It won't be a decorative, picturesque dream world, or about public-school lovers with no sexual organs ... [Oberon's fairies were all male and Titania's all female] ... Just as Titania has refused Oberon her bed, so that diktat runs all through the fairy world. The wood will be full of sexual tension ... It won't remind you of a mythical Athens, but of fundamentalist society in the vice-grip of Puritanism and arranged marriage. That's the world Shakespeare was exploring.[58]

When Titania begins her amour with furry-eared Bottom, the effect is usually a little less erotic than the teddy bears' picnic. Not in Michael Boyd's bold and brilliant revival ... Multiple orgasms are clearly occurring in the bed hovering above the stage ... When Josette Simon's squirming, leggy fairy queen tells Daniel Ryan's post-coital Bottom that one of her ogling attendants will 'fetch thee new nuts', her hand is on a part of his body that suggests she does not just mean tasty acorns.[59]

A party from a local Catholic school walked out of this production at the interval. Their teacher felt it was unsuitable for children, declaring that 'The production has driven a horse and carriage through our school's religious and sex education policies.' The tabloids headlined: 'Sir Leads Walkout as Bard Sex Shocks Kids' (*Mirror*) and 'Children Shocked by Shakespeare in Lust' (*Daily Mail*).

Bottom strolls his way between the world of reality, theatricality and the supernatural. His transformation gives the traditional hobby horse of the May Day celebration an ironic twist. The hobby horse combined the ritualized promise of communal renewal and regeneration through the hybridization of man and beast. Deriving from pagan origins, he symbolized fecundity and continuity. In Elizabethan London, records show that the hobby horse was known at Midsummer pageants and at other seasons, in church, city and court activities. Bottom's transformation, which Jan Kott found both 'fascinating and repulsive', has gone comically wrong – instead of being as virile as a beast and a beautiful as a human, it has worked the other way round. The nature of his 'translation' turns Titania's desires from something potentially dark into something comic.

There is a tendency for people to assume that because a play contains fairies and magical elements that it has been written for children. This was not true in Shakespeare's day when a belief in the supernatural pervaded all ages and classes of society. Applauded by most critics for its inventiveness, Michael Boyd's production did have its critics who felt that the overtly sexual reading of the dream, which began for the RSC with Peter Brook, had become old hat. It appeared as though the *Dream* had come full circle, and that audiences were looking forward to the next radical and imaginative rethink of this complex play. They found it with Tim Supple's extraordinary multilingual Indian production for Dash Arts in 2006, at once a homage to Brook and a brilliant reinvention of the play for a multicultural, globalized world.

THE DIRECTOR'S CUT: INTERVIEWS WITH MICHAEL BOYD, GREGORY DORAN AND TIM SUPPLE

Michael Boyd, born in 1955, trained as a director at the Malaya Bronnaya Theatre in Moscow. He then worked at the Belgrade Theatre in Coventry and the Sheffield Crucible before founding his own company, the Tron in Glasgow. He became an Associate Director of the RSC in 1996, coming to prominence with his millennial staging of the three parts of *Henry VI* and *Richard III* in the company's 'This England' cycle of history plays, which won him an Olivier award for Best Director. In 2003, he took over as Artistic Director, achieving a notable success in 2006–07 with his ambitious Complete Works Festival, whereby all Shakespeare's plays were staged in Stratford-upon-Avon over the course of a year, some by the RSC and others by visiting companies. His controversial *Midsummer Night's Dream*, with Josette Simon as Hippolyta/Titania and Daniel Ryan as Bottom, was staged in 1999.

Gregory Doran, born in 1958, studied at Bristol University and the Bristol Old Vic theatre school. He began his career as an actor, before becoming Associate Director at the Nottingham Playhouse. He played some minor roles in the RSC ensemble before directing for the company, first as a freelance, then as Associate and subsequently Chief Associate Director. His productions, several of which have starred his partner Antony Sher, are characterized by extreme intelligence and lucidity. He has made a particular mark with several of Shakespeare's lesser-known plays and the revival of works by his Elizabethan and Jacobean contemporaries. His 2005 *Midsummer Night's Dream* for the RSC featured Amanda Harris as Titania, Joe Dixon as Oberon, Jonathan Slinger as the Puck and Malcolm Storry as Bottom.

Tim Supple, born in 1963, studied at Cambridge University. As director of the Young Vic, he pioneered a style of theatrical narrative, often in the form of dramatizations of classic stories (such as Kipling's *Jungle Book* and a selection of tales from Ovid's *Metamorphoses* in the versions of Ted Hughes), that was simple and direct but also full of improvisation and innovative stage effect. He directed an RSC production of *The Comedy of Errors* on tour in India, which introduced him to Indian styles of theatre, story-telling and popular entertainment. This gave him the idea of recruiting an Indian company to play *A Midsummer Night's Dream*. The resulting production for his own company Dash Arts (funded by the British Council), in a mixture of many Indian tongues as well as English, was a global triumph and a high point of the visiting work featured in the RSC 2006–07 Complete Works Festival.

A wood outside Athens where some very English artisans rehearse their amateur play. Theseus and Hippolyta jumping out of Greek mythology one moment and the English folklore figure of Robin Goodfellow the next. A production history that runs from the bare thrust stage of Shakespeare to elaborate Victorian scenography complete with trees and even live rabbits to Peter Brook's white cube with circus trapeze. How did you and your designer set about imagining and realizing the world of *A Midsummer Night's Dream*?

MB: Tom Piper and I wanted to move from a cold oppressive world (with bad weather) to a much happier and more colourful place, via the comic and disturbing challenge of the wood. We were also very keen to thrust the action as far as possible into the same room as the audience while staying within the sightlines of the old Royal Shakespeare Theatre. What emerged was a smooth raised egg shape rising over the front of the stalls and enclosed by a seamless, seemingly doorless, curved wooden wall at the back of the curve. This closed off the proscenium, put pressure on the space, and also acted as a natural loudspeaker, thus enabling the actors to play freely with the whole range of their voices.

Athens was populated by grey, buttoned-up people in buttoned-up coats, and it snowed. Fur hats and a general air of frigid obedience gave an Eastern European feel to the opening scenes. Even the mechanicals wore identical grey suits, but it was Bottom's vitality and imagination that produced the first crack in this imposed closed order. He imagines and embodies the heroic gesture of 'hold or cut bowstrings' so vividly that his mimed Robin Hood longbow shoots a real arrow into the curved (Berlinesque) wall. The wall opens and a buttoned-up lady walks out of a door as poppies start to grow from the floor in a riot of red all over the stage. Colour has arrived and Bottom runs away. The lady starts picking the poppies and is now being followed by the bowler-hatted, white-gloved Philostrate, who has also 'escaped' through the hole in the wall. Philostrate harasses the woman in an increasingly sexual manner until they fight, rip each other's clothes apart and reveal themselves to be Robin and Peaseblossom.

The world of the court now rapidly transforms, costumes morph and reveal highly coloured linings. So the world of the fairies bursts out from within the oppressive world of the court, forming two highly charged teams of male and female. Oberon and his men/boys literally burst the floor open with their violent entrances through traps, further smashing the smooth ellipse, and trapping Peaseblossom.

GD: I suppose the first thing you have to acknowledge about the *Dream* is that there are three or four very distinct strata. I began by being aware that in order to create a fantastical world, I wanted to root the real world in a very specific and mundane reality. We began with the world of the rude mechanicals. They've got very specific jobs; there's a weaver, a carpenter, a bellows-mender, etc., and they work on Athenian stalls. They live under a very strict authority – if they frighten the ladies with the lion they think they will all be hanged, so it's not a cosy society. We wanted to make them real people. I think the problem for me in dressing them in Elizabethan or some sort of abstract costume is that you need a point of departure for the abstraction of the fairies, and you can make the mechanicals exotic by putting them in Elizabethan costume. I wanted them to be absolutely recognizable working men. I walked up and down Chapel Market in Islington and looked at the market stalls and the kind of people that worked there. It seemed to me that by making the mechanicals very ordinary, real people they would be funnier and the relationships between them more truthful.

From that point we had to leap off to find out what the world of the court was. In the court you find that the society run by Duke Theseus is again a very dangerous society, in which if girls don't obey their fathers they might be executed or be forced to join a convent. Whenever I come to direct a Shakespeare play, I try to read it as if for the first time, as if the ink is still wet on the page. You draw from that, without necessarily trying to tie everything up, all the various resonances that you can. Athens felt to me a bit like Greece under the Colonels, so I began to look at that as a reference point – a totalitarian dictatorship.

You have within that another whole strand with Duke Theseus. Shakespeare is like some great hydra. You manage to find a setting or locale or reality for one bit and then an extra head plops out and says 'Well, you've forgotten me.' By looking at the Theseus – Hippolyta story and seeing whether it married, we began to see Theseus as a normal, ordinary, upper-class aristocrat who plays out the fantasy that he has captured the Amazonian queen. It's the first bit of fantasy in the play. We began the play with a fight between two armed warriors, in Greek armour, crashing through an extraordinary sword-and-shield fight, which one of them then won. When the victor took off their helmet it turned out to be a woman. So you have the Amazonian warrior element of Hippolyta, and this time Theseus enjoyed being beaten by the warrior queen. Then they quickly got into their ordinary clothes for the arrival of Philostrate and Egeus. So there was a fantasy element in the role playing that they were doing. I see very little other element of their, as it were, mythological status. When they are alone in Act 4 and start talking about being on a bear hunt with my kinsmen Hercules and Cadmus we decided that it was their own fantasy; again, to root them as real people in a real context, as the lovers were real people in a real context. It is more surprising if a fairy appears to somebody who is absolutely real and literal.

That was our starting point, and then the world of the forest became a sort of wasteland. When Shakespeare talks about forests we are in danger of thinking of pretty woodland glades, whereas I think what he is talking about is a wilderness into which people go and are changed by the experience. We created a rather sinister forest, which was a kind of forest and also a junk heap, with lots of detritus that had been chucked away by the world. The rude mechanicals brought a market stall into the forest which they were going to use as their little stage to rehearse, and a supermarket trolley to carry the props. And the fairies leapt from that.

TS: Our approach was very practical at first: how do we suggest the journey from court to street to forest back to the street and then court? And how do we travel within the forest – how do we suggest different locations, experiences, emotions? And how, when we return to the court, can it feel different than it was? We discussed, sketched and tried out many things in rehearsal but we were always heading for something light, simple and suggestive. Something that could move and change with ease but with magical sensation. Before rehearsals began we had decided that the play should begin with a clean image – that the court should play on silk, and against a huge wall of white paper that would look like something classical and solid. We knew that we wanted to pull the silk off the floor, like a tablecloth, and play the street scene on earth. And we knew that we wanted the fairies to enter the play by bursting through the paper and that the torn back wall would suggest the lines and shape of the forest. We knew also that the gradual mess that would be created as the paper was ripped and trampled and the earth churned up during Acts 2 and 3 would naturally create the turbulence we felt to be at the heart of Shakespeare's forest. Indeed, we felt that the forest should transform from scene to scene with the shifting psychological experience of the characters and that we wanted this to be achieved by the simplest, playful means, with the fairies and Robin always central to how things change. The fairies' whirling sticks would create the dangerous war-zone of 2.1; the fairies would climb and dance up silks and ropes to sing Titania to sleep in 2.2; the fairies provide a playful, benign forest for the mechanicals in 3.1 before Robin leads a vicious attack and the same forest turns into a nightmare. We knew that Act 4 would begin with the clean simplicity of dawn – all mess removed, while Act 5 would mark a return to silk, but now red and rich and sensual. At all times we were aiming for a design that would open the audience's imagination while providing a concrete enough sense of each place and world – court, street and forest; mortal and immortal. In rehearsal we were inspired by the place where we worked – Tamil Nadu. Our red earth, natural wooded grid, large leaves and many other details came from there. In the costumes we worked hard to articulate three distinct worlds that would connect with the eternal folk play-within-the-play while resonating with a modern audience. The aristocrats' clothes trod a fine line between mythic dress and modern cloth; the mechanicals were always to be absolutely real – as one would find them on the streets of Calcutta; the fairies were most elusive for they had to be many things – playful, malign, light, potent – as they are Nature itself. The binding aesthetic was always India. It was not to be set in India but to arise from India: India as it was and as it is.

If the Chamberlain's Men's property store was like that of their rivals under Philip Henslowe, they might have had a wheel-on 'bank' for Titania to lie upon, but meeting 'by moonlight' in the outdoor Elizabethan theatre could not have been achieved by fancy lighting effect. Where in your production did you rely most on modern theatre technology and where did you just let the language and the audience's imagination do the work?

MB: We flew Bottom and Titania in the bed, we brought Oberon from the substage up to Titania's raised bed with phallic hydraulics, but this was a very simple production, which expressed itself in words, behaviour, costume, and through [movement coach] Liz Ranken's sexually charged dance rituals.

4. Tim Supple's wood: behind, the bamboo frame through which the fairies burst; around, the twine with which Robin entangled the lovers.

GD: I do think it is important to release the audience's imagination, to allow them to be complicit. In receiving the language they should not be too distracted. We did create a starlit sky. There was a puppet-theatre technique we used. Snout had a stall where he was selling greasy hot dogs and falafel, an Athenian greasy spoon. The light on his frying dish was projected against the back wall of the mechanicals' market stall lock-up, so you got a sense of greasy onions and sausages, etc., projected against the back wall. We used that image but made it rather beautiful in the forest. Steve Tiplady, from Little Angel, by pouring ink and then oil into a Pyrex dish and then putting it onto an overhead projector, created a night sky. All the oil distributed into tiny bubbles, and when you projected that onto the screen you had an astonishing galaxy of stars, which looked absolutely like a night sky. All you then had to do was run your finger through the Pyrex dish and you got fantastic shooting stars. We allowed ourselves to use that, but you were always aware

5. Titania (Josette Simon) and Bottom (Daniel Ryan) in Michael Boyd's sexually-charged RSC production.

that it was 'rough magic', if you like. And when you saw the fairies with their huge wings you knew that it was a shadow-play trick. So we did allow ourselves quite a lot of fun with that, but tried always to keep the actor and the spoken word at the forefront. We were probably not as rigorous as the way Peter Brook did it when he created the white box, but that was thirty or forty years ago, and I think bringing back a bit of theatre magic, without it becoming a Victorian scene with white rabbits, could still create an image in the audience's mind of night and of the forest being a dangerous place.

We continued the sense of the fairies being obsessed with the adults. In the way that Titania and Oberon are obsessed with the changeling boy, the fairies themselves become obsessed with the lovers in the forest. They became the bushes and the briars through which the lovers scrambled. Basically they denuded the lovers as they went through the scene, by holding their clothes as they tore them off them. We thought hard about what a forest was and what it would be like going through a forest at night and we created that experience not with bushes and briars but by using the fairies. In the scene where Puck takes Demetrius and Lysander off to fight 'cheek by jowl' we made the boys' trips through the forest quite difficult by giving them a lot of physical action to get through the groups of fairies, over the top of them and round about them.

With such a huge space, particularly in a proscenium arch, you have to fill that picture frame in some way. You can do it with lights and things other than just physical lumps of scenery. We didn't have very much scenery. Effectively we just kept the space clear and allowed the actors to fill that space. I did have a large globe moon, which was a very interesting element. As soon as we put a moon on the stage, we followed the stages of the moon through the play and realized that something very strange is going on. Hippolyta at the beginning says that in four days' time the moon will be like 'a silver bow / New-bent in heaven', talking about the transitional phases of the moon – there is going to be a new moon in four days' time, but until then no moon. But Lysander seems to think there will be a moon 'Tomorrow night, when Phoebe doth behold / Her silver visage in the wat'ry glass'; and then as soon as we are in the forest Oberon says 'Ill met by moonlight, proud Titania', so instead of there being no moon at all, as is the case in the first scene, suddenly there is a moon. Either Shakespeare is not being literal or he's being very precise, and people have worked out exactly what that means. The moon to us presided over the play. In fact it moved during the show and was lit in different ways, just as the physical globe of the moon is always there in the sky but is lit in from different angles by the sun. We lit it in very different ways during the piece, and then allowed it to blossom into this huge flower which provided the final antidote to the love-in-idleness: 'Dian's bud o'er Cupid's flower / Hath such force and blessèd power': so we were following through a large abstract idea of the moon and chastity and also its relationship to sex and fecundity. I think that is a key link.

TS: Our only use of modern technology is in the lighting – which is very important to the production – and in the microphones that lift the levels of our live musical instruments to fill the large theatres in which we play. On the other hand, we never rely simply on language and the audience's imagination alone. However minimal, there is always some intervention from the set, the light or the music to help define a moment. There is a very interesting way in which the most traditional theatre practice – still alive in India today – meets with contemporary imaginative theatre approaches in the West. In our production a limited set of resources – musical instruments played live or sticks, rope, silks and elastic or even a rubber tyre – have provided limitless possibilities of imaginative play. In a way, we are trying to combine the playfulness and freedom of children with the refined, layered sophistication of the wisdom and experience found in the text. In 3.2, when the four lovers dissolve into a deadly fight of jealous rivalry, our Puck gleefully weaves a web of elastic around them in which they become entangled and flail to the point of desperation. This is certainly an addition to the language and a stimulant to the audience's imagination. It suggests another shape to the forest floor, but it also plays a very simple trick on the lovers – one that a child could conceive of, but that also plays with their entangled love with the force of Cupid. This is in fact what the mechanicals themselves discover in 3.1: how do you 'bring moonlight into a chamber'? You get a man to suggest moonshine with a torch and bush! Ingenious, playful and symbolic.

In what sense was your Hippolyta an Amazonian captive? And how seriously did you take Oberon's assertion that Theseus (led on by Titania) is a serial rapist?

MB: Josette Simon has great beauty and dignity and was dressed elegantly as Hippolyta, but chastely. She and Oberon stood far apart as their forthcoming wedding was announced to choreographed applause. Disharmony lay beneath the optimistic rhetoric in the summer snow.

GD: We felt Theseus was actually a very ordinary man who had this fantasy. Oberon and Titania see them in mythological terms as fantasies that they want to play out. Oberon's description seems to have no relationship to Theseus at all. Theseus himself has a very strange attitude to any kind of imaginative capacity, finding it all a bit suspicious. It seemed to us that that was Oberon and Titania creating a sort of mythological context for the play. I think you could see in my production that there is a relationship to that myth, but that it was another layer of fantasy. I don't think it helps to see Theseus as a serial rapist.

TS: Shakespeare is enigmatic, or very open, about both Hippolyta and Theseus. Who knows how much this was deliberate or the mark of unfinished work? But the most interesting approach is to assume that it was deliberate and, rather than fixing the nature of Hippolyta's captivity or Theseus' character, leave it as open as possible. We know that they have fought and that Theseus has won and we know that they get married. We don't know how Hippolyta feels about this. Her first words are ambiguous and could be convincingly played as both willing compliance and biting resentment. When decisions have to made, we tried to make just enough to bring a story to life and to create the sense of journey and change that all good stories need. In our production, Hippolyta has lost a war, agreed to marry, but has no love for Theseus. An Amazonian queen, she has no voice in Athens' court. Her journey is to come to terms with the situation she is in: his journey is to win her love – not through conquest or through spectacle. This occurs in 4.1 when his flexibility leads him to champion the young lovers over Egeus and the law. What has occurred to bring about this change? We know nothing about Theseus and Hippolyta after 1.1. The process of change is surely to be found in the forest. Titania and Oberon are the continuation of the battle between Hippolyta and Theseus and their turbulent, ferocious fight over marital power, sexual ownership, a child and the world that they are responsible for, is the dream-catharsis that exorcizes and resolves the buried issues and frustrations between the two mortal monarchs. We have to take everything that one character says about another seriously, while remembering that it is only the perspective of one character. We would not be surprised if Theseus was a rapist – surely this is common to many powerful figures of myth? But we would not be surprised if Oberon is exaggerating in his jealousy and anger. What we can assume is that Theseus has yet to learn love in its tender, thoughtful, selfless sense. He must make the journey from absolute monarch-soldier who wins his wife on the battlefield to a man who knows love. He is given this by Oberon and Titania who sit beautifully poised between two modern notions, being both alter-egos and spirit-gods of love.

What's going on with all that business in which Oberon and Titania fight over the Indian boy? Some productions actually include the boy in the cast ...

MB: In my Crucible production the boy was played by Mumta Gupta, the gorgeous son of Nirmal Gupta, who ran by far the best curry house in Sheffield and loved the snooker. We had no onstage boy in Stratford, but his unconscious root might be the Child Christ whose mother the Virgin Mary has been so recently banished from English spirituality. Titania's account of disharmony has strong suggestions of an England out of joint following the Reformation.

GD: [*See GD's answer to the question about the fairies, pp. 145–6.*]

TS: Again, this is an enigmatic, or open, aspect of the play and one can either explain it clearly or leave it open. We chose the latter while never forgetting that it is at the heart of what they are arguing about and so must be essential to their very beings. We are told by Puck that Oberon wants the boy to be a special member of his followers – a scout or ranger. We can imagine that a little mortal child would be as special to a spirit as a spirit-child would be to a mortal. But it is hard to believe that this is all such a terrible fight is about. In the argument between them in 2.1 we can surmise that Oberon is furious that his request is being denied, and perhaps the boy has become a symbol of the love and sexual partnership that she is denying him. 'Am I not thy Lord?!' he thunders when she tries to leave his company again. Is the boy the battleground for marital power within which sexual availability and fidelity is the real issue? This is possible, but does not feel quite deep or rich enough to enter the bloodstream of such a play of wonderful humanity. It is striking what emerges in Titania's speech when she is pushed. The boy is a child of a woman who loved her and with whom she shared tenderness, humour and friendship. The woman died, and for her sake, Titania has made the boy her own. Is the potent issue here the fact that, being immortals, Titania and Oberon cannot have children? In a play in which all the characters yearn to be other than they are, is it Titania and Oberon's yearning to have a child, to be a family? This is not so fanciful: at the end of the play they come to the marriage beds to bless the sexual union of the three couples and the children that they will have. If the ending requires some profound union between all the characters of the play, this might indeed make a deep connection between the immortal and mortal worlds. One of the toughest challenges presented by the boy in the play is simply to make it clear – a common phrase one hears from audiences at productions of the *Dream* is: 'What exactly are Oberon and Titania fighting about?' It can be useful and interesting to have the boy in the show, as we do, to help establish the character firmly in the story. However, even this cannot make the argument easily clear to all watching. Perhaps, like all marriages, the exact issue in a falling out can never be clear to outsiders. Or perhaps the most important clue is in the mystery itself. A great concern of the play is the mystery of the immortal or spirit world. We yearn to touch it. In love and art (theatre) we can glimpse it, but it will remain a mystery. A dream.

Though it requires some very quick costume changes, many productions double Theseus with Oberon and Hippolyta with Titania. Did yours? Why? Why not? Gains and losses, discoveries?

MB: We were bound to double them as our premise was that the woods were a transforming agent on Athenian life, permitting the release of repressed or taboo ideas and urges. The biggest single gain was the moving and dangerous moment when Bottom approached Hippolyta in the Bergamasque dance. Both of them half understood what they had each 'dreamed' the night before. The humanizing of Nick Jones as Theseus through Oberon was also powerful.

GD: We didn't. The reason was that it has actually become the norm to double them. It's fine for Oberon and Titania, but the worry I had was that Hippolyta and Theseus are rather diminished. You stop regarding them in their own right, and I wanted to look at them in their own capacities and at their own agendas, to try to understand who they are. There's a physical moment which is very difficult, because you have to have an extraordinarily quick change when they go off and come straight back on again, which seems to indicate to me that it was not the original purpose to double them. Rather than effect a clever quick change I decided not to have that at all and to try and look at them in their own right. I think that brought distinct advantages theatrically. One problem is that, when you get to the moment when Oberon and Titania are reconciled, which I think is an incredibly important moment in the play, then that moment becomes loaded with the practical issue of how you are going to do the quick change. When the fairies come back on right at the end of the play after Theseus and Hippolyta and the lovers have all gone off to bed, and there is a sense of the play coming to an end, I think not doubling the roles increases the audience's sense of wonder and delight. There's a growing sense of joy there, and I love the fact that Oberon and Titania do come back to enter the palace. The danger is that if Theseus and Hippolyta do another quick change you are more aware of the quick change than you are of the wonder of the moment. There's a sense of benediction at the end of the play. It shows it clearly wasn't just a dream after all. The fairies' role has been re-established as somehow preservers of the natural order and their benediction of the mothers and the newlyweds was somehow more special without the doubling.

TS: We did double Theseus with Oberon and Hippolyta with Titania as well as Philostrate with Puck. Even Egeus appears in the forest as a spirit. It seemed absolutely natural to do this on the page and it feels absolutely natural in performance. The reasons are numerous. The perfect structure of the play invites it: the mortal court disappears from view for the middle three acts, leaving its key actors idle if they are not to reappear as the spirit-court. Without this doubling, Theseus and Hippolyta have no process of change or travel: the doubling creates a rich physical and psychological experience at the heart of the play. The core meaning of the play lies in transformation and the forest is the place of change. The lovers transform with wild and released ferocity into sexual animals. Bottom of course transforms into the ultimate sexual beast – the compliant ass. Becoming Titania and Oberon is the transformation undergone by Hippolyta and Theseus. As the spirit-monarchs, they too are released from the restraining forces of civilized society. They can fight their way with no holds barred through the painful, turbulent forest of sexual jealousy, marital power and mutual frustration. Like all classic folktales, the time and place of transformation is elsewhere and must be forgotten to the conscious mind. Bottom cannot hold on to the memory of his experience in the forest, nor can the lovers. How much more rich is this sense of dream if it is common to all the characters in the play? Hippolyta and Theseus' dream is to have been Titania and Oberon. This makes the stage one and binds the audience into a sensation of dream: 'That you have but slumbered here / While these visions did appear.' What losses there might be is hard to guess at – one would have to play the play the other way to discover. The most obvious loss would be a greater sense of concrete, discreet character in each mortal and each immortal. One might gain a sense of travel – of leaving the court, the city and entering another, very different world. It would allow extreme differences in casting. One could even play with the two worlds colliding more often. Indeed, we can surmise that in

Shakespeare's time the mechanicals doubled with the fairies. This completes the dream, the surrealism of the mortal world becoming the immortal world. However, we definitely wanted mechanicals who would bring a reality to the stage and who would convince as working men from India's streets. This demanded a very different kind of performer and physical personality to those we cast as fairies. Having two different groups produced a vivid contrast between them and created a rich human canvas. It also allowed two wonderful events of meeting: 3.1 and the end.

Hermia and Helena are sharply differentiated, not least by their differing height, but sometimes the boys seem indistinguishable – there are moments when even seasoned playgoers can be hard put to remember who is in love with whom at which moment. That's partly the Puck's fault, of course, but would you say that the director needs to work especially hard to help actors realize Demetrius and Lysander distinctively?

MB: There's no excuse for confusing the characters of Lysander and Demetrius. Lysander is clearly a passionate rebel, prone to fits of melancholy. His vivid sense of mortality and his wooing techniques bring readily to mind the young John Donne: the young outsider courtier of the wrong persuasion. He's one of many trainee Hamlets. Demetrius, on the other hand, is a trainee Laertes. He has a passion in him, but it is buried, and takes second place to the main chance. The *Dream* could, in one sense, be subtitled 'The Awakening and Education of Demetrius'. He's the one lover who is truly and permanently transformed by the experience, and it is a good thing that he ends up a little more like Lysander.

GD: I think there is a distinct psychology behind all of them. Hermia and Helena are not just distinguished by their heights. Hermia is this spoilt little princess, who has always been the apple of her important father's eye, who has lived this very privileged existence and has had everything she wants, including the love of Lysander. She's a very determined little madam. I think she uses Lysander, who at the beginning of the play you can absolutely understand as the person that Hermia's father would not want to hang around his daughter. He's a bit of a wastrel. We had him physically sloppier. He's interested in love and the language of love. He's a sort of philosopher in his own mind, whereas Demetrius *is* the man Hermia's father wants him to marry. He is a city-type, a Hooray Henry. The advantage of having the boys in modern dress is that you can have certain signifiers for an audience. If Demetrius is dressed rather uptight, neatly cut hair, city suit, the Man Most Likely To, then you can distinguish him very clearly from Lysander, who wears rather romantic sloppy clothes and has long hair. Hermia is the princess. Helena is paranoid about her height and has rather low self-esteem. What the forest does is expose those paranoias. Hermia, who has always had love and just had to click her fingers for it to come to her, is suddenly abandoned, loved by neither of the men and left wandering around the forest by herself. I think that's very frightening for her. I don't think she's ever had to fall back on her own resources like that before. Helena is a bit of a masochist who has fallen comfortably into the position of playing the victim in life. Her problem is partially that she enjoys playing the victim. She says 'But herein mean I to enrich my pain.' It's an almost masochistic enjoyment of not being loved, proving that she is not worthy of love by chasing the wrong partner. Yet in the forest she finds herself being chased and adored by two men. Initially she finds it rather disturbing – they must be joking – and then she finds that there are certain advantages, and a certain power struggle evolves because of that. Lysander might be a bit soppy but he does hold true to his love. The revelation at the end comes when Demetrius admits that he has behaved badly, and from being a very arrogant man he becomes a very humble man. All of them have their true selves exposed in the forest. A mirror is held up exposing who they really are and it's very disturbing to see, but they come out of the forest with a better sense of vision. Their vision might be blurry initially, but ultimately they see each other and themselves much more clearly as a result of the night in the forest.

TS: As usual, Shakespeare sits finely poised between ancient and modern theatrical tastes with very interesting results. Actually the two boys are quite distinct in their actions and words – and they are different to each other both before and after the flower. Lysander is an idealist: a love warrior. His cult is love as he has read, thought and dreamt of it. He shows courage and the instincts of an adventurer in his pursuit of fidelity: suggesting elopement for marriage and restraining his lust for Hermia in the forest when she calls on him to do so. The flower of course reveals his other side: with Helena he releases his lust, ferocity and cruelty. It becomes urgent for him to have Helena, destroy Demetrius and crush Hermia.

Demetrius begins the play as the unreliable, opportunistic outsider of the four. He has loved Helena and ditched her, leaving her distraught, having transferred his desire on to Hermia despite her clear commitment to Lysander. He does not share the trysts and tales referred to by the other three. His reaction to their flight is wild: he will catch and kill Lysander just as Hermia is killing him. He threatens Helena with savagery and rape if she does not leave him alone. He tries to seduce Hermia when she is clearly distraught – allowing her to believe that he has killed Lysander. The effect of the flower is to allow him to worship Helena – he becomes less obsessed with seduction and more with defending her, in his eyes, against the false love of Lysander. After the calming, transforming sleep of the dark hours before dawn, this tangle of feelings is transformed into the deep, rich, devotional love he declares publicly in 4.1. These differences in word and deed must all be fully explored and exploited and made available to an audience. However, in performance the differences are superficial and the two characters remain stubbornly interchangeable. On the one hand I tend to agree with Jan Kott that there is core meaning here. The kind of love that concerns Shakespeare in the play, and in the forest especially, is not the romantic love that tells us that one true partner awaits us as in the final credits of the Hollywood Rom-Com. This is the tougher, more truthful face of young love when a partner can switch in the course of a night. When one's passion for one partner can evaporate in the dark when encouraged to turn its head to another. It is no villainy in Demetrius that his 'shower of oaths did melt' when it felt 'some heat' from Hermia. It is no villainy in Hermia either. It is just desire. And the *Dream* is about that part of love that is desire and the forest is the arena where desire can finally rule, unrestrained by family, responsibility, fidelity, marriage or time. In such a place, one partner is much like another and in our heart of hearts this is the truth we feel when we glance at stranger after stranger and wonder. In these moments of our life – especially in our youth – many partners are possible and anything can happen. On the other hand, the similarity we feel in the two is a result of their theatrical ancestry. The four lovers are in part developments of the lovers of *commedia dell'arte*, struggling through trials, largely created by a difficult father (Egeus). The stories, actions and expression of these lovers were very much to type and the scene between Hermia and Lysander at the end of 1.1 is especially influenced by the genre. Shakespeare's genius is to retain enough of the genre to appeal to his audience but to discover enough unique psychology in each character to allow them to live for modern audiences. His further genius is to create a group of six working men who, though less explored and revealed than his aristocratic lovers, are actually more individually defined.

And the girls: do we need them to feel real pain, real fear, not just of rejection but of rape?

MB: Yes. The woods are no less hilarious for being terrifying.

GD: I think that's right. The comedy of the play has to come out of a reality. It does descend into a fight, but that's not funny if they are not real people. I think there are moments of incredible revelation and shock. Hermia turns to Lysander and says 'What, can you do me greater harm than hate?' If you just treat these as funny scenes and funny characters and don't investigate them properly, they won't be funny. But they are funny if you have rooted their desires in reality. Helena's sense of victimization is actually deeply disturbing. She says 'Use me but as your spaniel'. That girl needs therapy! Unless you get into the reality of that neurosis, the psychological abstraction of the forest doesn't work.

TS: Of course: real everything! Pain, fear, abandonment, rape, but most of all terror in the face of themselves. Where do they end up by 3.2? Helena with no self-esteem, wishing only that 'sleep, that sometimes shuts up sorrow's eye / Steal me a while from mine own company.' Hermia, abandoned by best friend and devoted lover, trying to rip out Helena's eyes. The forest confronts each character with their most secret desire and fear of themselves. And surely this portrait would not be true if it did not include at least one moment in which Hermia did not want Demetrius and Helena Lysander? Helena cannot have entirely fabricated her image of Hermia sending out 'some heat' to Demetrius. And the flower juice is not, of course, a magical potion but a force of super-nature, as simply symbolic as Cupid's arrow. It brings about what is in our hearts.

Robin Goodfellow is a kind of stage manager, isn't he? Shakespeare loved writing parts of that kind (Iago, Prospero and Ariel, the Duke in *Measure for Measure*). Were there particular moments in your production that emphasized this aspect of the Puck's role?

MB: Puck would make a disastrous stage manager. He's much more of a Bottom than a stage manager. His egotistical lust for messing about in human lives is only matched by Bottom's egotistical urge to play every part in life. Iago may have liked to think of himself as Puck, but he was in fact a much meaner-spirited, smaller character. Aidan McArdle physically manipulated the lovers like a drunken Tadeusz Kantor [the revolutionary Polish artist and theatre director]. He rode them, he beat them, and emptied buckets of earth on them. He has more uncomplicated, unguilty relish than either Prospero, Ariel or the duke.

GD: Yes. As all the fairies become obsessed with the humans, he of course becomes obsessed with the rude mechanicals. He not only messes up the love potion, deliberately or otherwise, he also thoroughly enjoys involving himself in the play and turning Bottom into a literal ass. In a way you don't have to emphasize the stage manager role because it's very clearly there.

TS: Yes, many. Philostrate starts the production, walking slowly to the front centre and playing a strange, singing stone that starts the whole dream off. He sits at the front and watches the mechanicals in 1.2, transforming in front of our eyes into Puck as the stage transforms into the forest. He orchestrates the violent entanglement of the lovers in 3.2 by spinning a web of elastic around them and he signals both the start and the end of the interval. As Philostrate he sounds the hunting horns that wake Titania and Oberon up into Hippolyta and Theseus and, also as Philostrate, he makes the stage fit for Act 5. In the blessing dance he transforms again to Puck while Hippolyta and Theseus are transforming into their spirit alter-egos. This all, of course, leads to the most wonderful fruition in the play when Puck offers the audience a simple understanding of the complex picture that has unfurled in front of their eyes: the actors are the shadows, the play a series of visions and the experience of the event was itself only a dream.

Quince, Bottom and friends: their play has got to be bad, but you don't want the theatre audience to condescend to them, as some members of the onstage audience do during the performance of 'Pyramus and Thisbe'. How did you deal with this problem, how conceive the play-within-the-play?

MB: We always remembered that the mechanicals were a loving grotesque of Shakespeare's own chosen profession, and ours. The naivety of Quince's play and the mechanicals' stagecraft is just a comic rendering of the absurdity of our attempts to capture life in play form. Their imagination and their open hearts more than make up for their mistakes. They are the classic comic apologia to a potentially offended courtly audience: 'Don't arrest us or close down our play: we're just a bunch of humble actors, who are a threat to nobody.'

GD: The rude mechanicals are intending to do the play as well as they can, they're just not very good. What we looked at, rather than a lot of comic business, was the moments we remembered from starting out in amateur theatre. Those moments of excruciating embarrassment when something unplanned happened. Costumes dropping off, or, as I remember in panto in Lancashire, the vicar's teeth falling out. It's in the attempts to cover it up and keep on doing it well that terrible things happen. That was what made it funny.

We looked at the dirty jokes, which are a crucial part of 'Pyramus and Thisbe', but are a very difficult part to play because the verbal jokes tend not to work. Terms like 'stones' and 'hole' don't quite register nowadays in the context of the play. We addressed that very specifically by making a costume go wrong. The chink has been demonstrated in the rehearsal in the forest as Snout holding his fingers to form a chink. But I don't think when it comes to the performance of the play in front of the duke that the chink being fingers allows the stones and hole jokes to work. So we imagined that Snout, in creating his wall costume – we used a laundry basket covered in lime and plaster, so he did look like a wall – had forgotten to provide a hole through which he could put his hand. So he had to lift it, which exposed his Y-fronts. As he turned to face Pyramus and Thisbe they were faced with either the front of the Y-fronts or the back of the Y-fronts, which led to the excruciating embarrassment of Flute and Bottom as they had to say these lines about kissing the wall's hole, or referring to his stones knit up 'with lime and hair'. It was their embarrassment about having to carry on, faced with this big red pair of Y-fronts, that produced the fun. But it was based on a real sense of the embarrassment of being on stage when something goes wrong, rather than trying to invent comic business which isn't really there.

TS: Firstly, does it have to be bad? Or if so, how bad? And in what way bad? I would only say for sure that it needs to be artless. It must be, truthfully, a play performed by people who have not done plays – apart from one who started the play thinking that he knows more than he does about plays and acting. But has not even Bottom undergone some change, some transformation? Certainly also the language of 'Pyramus and Thisbe' has many mistaken uses of

English and crude examples of rhyme, metre and vocabulary. But I am not sure how important the quality of the performance is. The most important questions that we asked about the play-within-the-play were the same as we would ask about any scene: what are they doing, for what end and with what result? To answer this we made the simple decision to take the mechanicals as seriously as any characters in the play. We thought of them, in detail, as traders and craftsmen. We observed all the details we could from the text of what might be their work, their lives, their social status, their relationship with each other and their relationship with theatre. And we looked for how all these details might change through the course of the story. We were trying to escape from one of the most odious (or 'odorous!') habits of the *Dream* in performance: to see the mechanicals as 'comic relief' and their play as an excuse for endless directorial and actorly invention of ways in which these thoughtful, struggling men can be made to look foolish or cute. We tried several versions of their 'Pyramus and Thisbe', each one an attempt to imagine just how they would do it given they have no money and little art, and indeed have had no time to rehearse as their first and last rehearsal was interrupted by Bottom's transformation. We thought about what kinds of theatre they would have seen – probably theatre from the street – and how this would inform their choices. Most of all, we thought about who they are and who they have become by the end of the play. In the end, our version has no mistakes, no invented business – rather, it attempts to reveal in a bare and honest way, the experiences of those six men performing at the wedding of the most powerful monarch in their universe.

In terms of theatre, I find their journey fascinating and moving and I feel that their version of 'Pyramus and Thisbe' is as interesting a passage about theatre as the players' visit to *Hamlet*'s Elsinore. Indeed it should be: Shakespeare has chosen to place it at the end. He has chosen it to be the climax of his action. After the performance there is the magnificent finale of the Bergamasque, the exit of the couples to their sexual union and then the blessing song and dance. This remarkable ending demands that the conclusion of the action before be of greater resonance and value than a bad play that makes us laugh. It needs to be, in some way, a conclusion. Perhaps an epiphany. Or at least an arrival. The mechanicals' journey from first meeting to performance via the forest is one in which they discover theatre for themselves. In their first scene they encounter the basic fears that anyone may hold about performance. Will they become foolish? Will their limitations be exposed? Most of all, will their performance scare their aristocratic audience and lead to their punishment? There is little collective instinct in this first scene. There is conflict between the writer/ director and the leading actor – a struggle for leadership – and there are individual issues and anxieties. In the forest this reaches a head. They confront the basic problems of theatre: how to reassure the audience that it is not real (prologue) and how to make moonlight and a wall appear in an indoor room. The imaginative solutions that first Quince, then Bottom, propose – that both can be symbolized, simply, by an actor – bring the group together. In the first rehearsal, Flute has to learn the very basic dynamics of drama. Bottom's transformation into an ass drives a juggernaut through the play rehearsals but will ultimately ignite inspiration into its core. Firstly, the other men realize how much they value him and how much the play meant to them all. They will express this eloquently in 4.2. Secondly, Bottom becomes the only mortal of the play to cross over to the other side – to become the lover of the Queen of the Fairies. Titania promises him that she will purge his mortal spirit so that he will 'like an airy spirit go'. This is fulfilled in the performance. When he awakes his wonder, and sense of the remarkable mystery that he has experienced, is immediately translated into artistic thinking: he will perform a ballad of his dream. When he returns to the group he has new dignity and poise. Now he can be truly believed as the natural leader he earlier imagined himself to be. In performance of the play he anchors a great achievement. They do it. And not only do they do it, each one of them masters some great challenge: Quince follows a disastrous first prologue with a cogent and passionate second; Snout is strong and dignified as Wall; Snug charms the ladies with eloquence and humility; Starveling over- comes terrible teasing to insist on his role; Flute takes on the female role with tremendous vigour. And Bottom is so inspired in his death that he imagines that his 'soul is in the sky'. However crude, however artless, surely something must occur, something must be stirred?

The workmen offer the aristocrats a play about the play we have just seen. In the dim recesses of their memory or dream, they and we must be somehow affected by the honesty and directness they bring to the centre of the experience.

6. Pyramus (Joy Fernandes), Wall (Umesh Jagtap) and Thisbe (Joyraj Bhattacharya) in Tim Supple's production.

Tell us about your Bottom: the largest part (!), the most foolish character, but in his way the wisest, certainly the most lovable, but it's crucial to avoid sentimentality towards him, isn't it? And the specific choice of how to do his ass's head: a pair of ears and maybe a comic nose is one thing, a fully realistic animal head quite another. What did you go for? And would you say that this costuming decision plays a major part in determining whether the stage-image of Bottom making love to Titania is essentially comical, politically subversive (a weaver making love to a queen!), or perverse and grotesque in the manner of Ovid's *Metamorphoses* (a beautiful woman having sex with a donkey)?

MB: Our Bottom opened the door to the transforming wood with the real force of his imaginative arrow. He and Puck were the *two* Lords of Misrule. He reminded Titania what happiness was, and provided an inspirational leader to the duke's Players. Daniel Ryan's Bottom's Pyramus was actually very good; it was just over-inventive and needed a stronger editor, a more forceful director, than Quince.

A full donkey's head (as I had in Sheffield) is too literal and restricts the actor and risks us losing contact with him for too long. Big ears and a powerful groin are the only essential elements. Shakespeare clearly intends to refer to primitive bestiality as well as to subversive Lord of Misrule in Bottom's love-making with Titania. We had one foolish teacher who walked his children out of the theatre and gained notoriety and a *Guardian* editorial defending us.

GD: I think with Bottom you have to have a sense of a good-natured braggart. He is absolutely determined to play the biggest part, and all the other parts, which could make him completely intolerable. But then he is faced with this extraordinary fantasy of being wooed by, presumably, the most beautiful, glamorous creature he has ever seen. I remember when I was just starting out as a director, I did the play in a Community College in upstate New York. I went to do a seminar on the play in the psychology department and somebody asked me if I felt it was suitable for the students. When I asked why, they said, 'Well, jealous husband makes wife have it off with donkey. Isn't that a rather disturbing message?' Of course that is true, in that there is a weirdly subversive sexual nonsense that goes on. But I think it's so funny because Bottom is who Bottom is. If you play with the element of the play's dark sexuality as being as psychologically complex and dangerous as that, I think you're in danger of tipping the whole play over. I think he plays it with a sort of wit and lightness. I think if you really investigate what Oberon has done, when Titania wakes up and realizes 'I just had it off with a donkey' then I don't think there would be any measure of reconciliation between them. There is an exuberant, primal, primitive joy about the whole thing. That's where it becomes a most fantastical dream: where things start morphing into different shapes and it becomes weird and wonderful. I think there is a darkness to it, but a Jan Kott level of darkness just topples the play.

TS: Yes. Bottom is the very core of the play. See above [pp. 141–3]!

The fairies: large or small? Cute or sinister? They've been Victorian children clad in gossamer, they've been doubles of the mechanicals. What were yours like?

MB: The fairies were dull, repressed courtiers let loose and strangely morphed and coloured.

GD: The way we approached the fairies was to deal with their abstraction after we had dealt with the reality of them as individuals. Puck seemed to us like he was losing his touch. He was unable any longer to make Oberon smile, because Oberon has been distracted by his obsession with the changeling boy, and Puck, I think, is jealous of that. We felt that the First Fairy saying 'Oh, you're that Puck character aren't you', was a bit like somebody saying 'Oh, you're that funny guy off the TV.' But Puck couldn't live up to that reputation any more. He was a bit like Tony Hancock or an old comedian whose jokes no longer work, who used to be great but suddenly it just isn't working for him. That was the beginning of our take on Puck. And Puck through the play regains Oberon's affection and revivifies as a fairy.

Similarly with Titania and Oberon, we needed to make sure that there was a real battle going on over the changeling boy, and a real sense of deep loss. It seems as through they can both have sex with human beings, but they can never have children. So the obsession with the changeling boy we thought was a very real obsession. Because I really wanted to focus attention on the changeling boy and his appeal to them, we made a Bunraku puppet of a lifesize toddler. If you want to have the changeling boy on the stage, children are immensely distracting. Even if they are good you still think they might fall over. Certainly what you couldn't do is have a child as young as the changeling boy is clearly meant to be. His mother, it seems, has only recently given birth. We wanted the child to have a presence and we decided that by having a puppet, somehow the fairies would appear real and the puppet a mortal.

That introduced a whole other element in the play, which was an element of fantasy. I developed a relationship with the Little Angel Theatre, having done *Venus and Adonis* with them, and they provided a very special magic. There were two elements of that. One was that I noticed how often the word 'shadow' is used in the play, and so felt shadow-play might be a fascinating element. We all know from shining a torch against your hand as a child and it making a great big scary shadow on the bedroom ceiling, that shadows can create huge and extraordinary things. Once we had worked out that language it allowed us, when the fairies first appear and are gathering the dewdrops, to have fairies with huge Arthur Rackham wings, who were absolutely the sort of fairies that we immediately think of as fairies. The fairies from the Conan Doyle hoax. We were able to have fairies with great big wings and then undermine that. They could present themselves in your imagination but then they could be very real too.

I was very interested by Shakespeare's use of scale. Apparently the fairies can crawl into an acorn cup, but then Titania can have sex with a human being, so there's a variety of scale there. We spent quite a lot of time looking at those extraordinary Victorian fairy paintings; the mad, rather disturbing ones of Richard Dadd; the Irish painter Daniel Maclise's extraordinary paintings; and the famous fairy paintings by Fuseli and Noel Paton. We looked at how painters can easily enjoy that variety of scale. There are paintings of fairies fighting with owls and bats on a monster scale. We wanted to play with that. The shadow element helped with that, as did the use of dolls. I remember finding a sack of my sisters' old dolls when we were clearing out while moving house, and the dolls had lost their hair and eyes; they were weird-looking things. I showed them to my sisters and they were repelled by them. They found them rather disturbing; these creatures that they had loved and that had become real for them as children were now these ghastly monsters. When Bottom was attended by the fairies they all had these dreadful old dolls, which they presented to him so that the fairies could land on his hand. I used them as if the fairies were invisible unless they showed the dolls. We played with the iconic idea of the fairy, and then we subverted that into something else.

We did want to make real the way that the dissension between Oberon and Titania has apparently turned the world upside down. So the rude mechanicals were constantly running through the rain. The seasons have altered. The world is uncannily changed. The 'forgeries of jealousy' speech seems to suggest global warming. There seems to be this terrifying prospect that the world has been somehow damaged and is out of kilter, and the weather itself is changing. We wanted to utilize that to get away from the sense of the forest as a twinkly, starry place.

7. Bottom (Malcolm Storry) in Gregory Doran's shopping trolley, with puppet fairies.

TS: We found the fairies the hardest characters to costume and tried several versions before the final costumes were created during the night between the dress rehearsal and opening performance in Delhi. But we never found them hard to play. We wanted to avoid all stylization and all decisions of one overall tone. We wanted the fairies to be as unpredictable as nature itself and free from all human psychology – especially restraint, morality, tactical thinking, guilt, responsibility, etc. We wanted creatures of pure action. In part they are distant cousins of harlequin, always playful, and in part they are purely physical forces like dancers or acrobats. How they are comes from what they do. In 2.1 they fight like vicious insects; in 2.2 they magically bind Titania's lair with a spell to keep her at peace and asleep then wrap Hermia and Lysander into their own chrysalis of sleep. In 3.1 they playfully provide a benign forest for the mechanicals made up of cane and cloth leaves and of fans and mops and nets. With Puck, they enjoy watching these strange mortals rehearse their play and then, like vicious children, they turn on the mechanicals and drive them mad by chasing them, a screeching assault, out of the forest. At Titania's demand, they attend to the new king of the fairies – Bottom, tying him up like Gulliver and leading him off to his lover's bed at the end of 3.1 in a wild bacchanalian dance. We wanted them to have the quality of Ovid's nymphs: immortal yet servile, free of all constraint yet shot-through with an ultimate tragic sense that we see but they cannot. Like insects that live for a day, they have no awareness of what they are missing, or how lucky they are. We felt that no single image or costume or characterisation could encapsulate all this. We had to leave the performer's body and the audiences' minds free to imagine and enjoy. Like Brook and his designer, Sally Jacobs, we chose to let them be performers. Only the performer him/herself, we felt, could be this thing and indeed the nearest we humans can get to these spirits is in performance. The trickery, the playfulness, the athleticism, the skill, the immaturity, the exotic wisdom, the viciousness, the delightfulness, the tenderness, the glimpse of immortality that will never last – all this is touched best by the performer. So our fairies wear as few clothes as possible, all black:

beautiful, simple clothes of performance that best suit their bodies and expose as much of their bodies as possible. Flesh and muscle, legs, backs and arms: these are the key elements of our shadows' costume.

So do you believe in fairies? More seriously, although this is traditionally the Shakespeare play that has the best chance of making children fall in love with Shakespeare in the theatre (was it like that for you?), some astute critics feel that it is a – perhaps the – central Shakespearean play, because it is such a profound exploration of theatre as dream, dream as theatre ... the ultimate embodiment of Coleridge's great remark about 'that willing suspension of disbelief for the moment, which constitutes poetic faith'.

MB: The poetic faith of Bottom was at the centre of our production, or at least our lantern through the forest of our expressed desires and fears and hates.

GD: The reason I enjoyed the elements of Puck and the masque and the shadow-play is because, as an audience, you know how the effect is being produced, but you are still amazed by it. If you could do extraordinary technological things, that wouldn't be as surprising. You would just be rather unemotionally engaged in the trickery. Whereas if you bring the audience in, and allow their imaginations to fly with what's happening in the play, I think it is the most wonderful act of theatre, because the play happens somewhere between the actor's imagination and the audience's imagination. It's that complicity which I think makes it such a special and such a blessed play. It is a great benediction.

It was surprising in many ways to us. Midsummer meant to the Elizabethans something very different to what it means to us today. To us it means Pimms, Wimbledon, long summer evenings and that sense of relaxation. To the Elizabethans it was a precarious time, when the crops were in the ground but the harvest hadn't arrived. If the weather was bad at that time it could spell disaster, because if the crops failed shortages could lead to all kinds of rural discontent.

It was a dangerous time. It was also a time of year when a portal opened between two worlds, and between Midsummer (St John's Eve) and the feast of St Peter the Apostle (23–29 June) was a time when fairies were supposed to be active. So there was a genuine sense of concern at that time. A Midsummer Night's dream to a modern audience sounds a time of relaxation and contentment. In Elizabethan terms it doesn't have quite those connotations of beauty and relaxation and ease. In approaching the play right from the start we began to realize that there were more things going on, and that they were of serious import.

TS: The *Dream* is, for me, too, the essential expression of Shakespeare's theatre. Playfully profound and profoundly playful; one foot in the ancient theatre and one foot marching toward the modern theatre; narratively exhilarating with time for no less than four major set-pieces of song and dance; perfectly constructed; a canvas of characters that range from the highest aristocrat to a tinker, with characters drawn in meticulous detail or magnificent generality, as befits the needs of the drama. And in the centre, the great invention of the fairies: immortals who are most like us. Ultimately the play shatters in its ability to draw all these elements together in an ending as central to the human experience as any work of theatre that I know of or can imagine.

SHAKESPEARE'S CAREER IN THE THEATRE

BEGINNINGS

William Shakespeare was an extraordinarily intelligent man who was born and died in an ordinary market town in the English Midlands. He lived an uneventful life in an eventful age. Born in April 1564, he was the eldest son of John Shakespeare, a glove-maker who was prominent on the town council until he fell into financial difficulties. Young William was educated at the local grammar in Stratford-upon-Avon, Warwickshire, where he gained a thorough grounding in the Latin language, the art of rhetoric and classical poetry. He married Ann Hathaway and had three children (Susanna, then the twins Hamnet and Judith) before his twenty-first birthday: an exceptionally young age for the period. We do not know how he supported his family in the mid-1580s.

Like many clever country boys, he moved to the city in order to make his way in the world. Like many creative people, he found a career in the entertainment business. Public playhouses and professional full-time acting companies reliant on the market for their income were born in Shakespeare's childhood. When he arrived in London as a man, sometime in the late 1580s, a new phenomenon was in the making: the actor who is so successful that he becomes a 'star'. The word did not exist in its modern sense, but the pattern is recognizable: audiences went to the theatre not so much to see a particular show as to witness the comedian Richard Tarlton or the dramatic actor Edward Alleyn.

Shakespeare was an actor before he was a writer. It appears not to have been long before he realized that he was never going to grow into a great comedian like Tarlton or a great tragedian like Alleyn.

Instead, he found a role within his company as the man who patched up old plays, breathing new life, new dramatic twists, into tired repertory pieces. He paid close attention to the work of the university-educated dramatists who were writing history plays and tragedies for the public stage in a style more ambitious, sweeping and poetically grand than anything which had been seen before. But he may also have noted that what his friend and rival Ben Jonson would call 'Marlowe's mighty line' sometimes faltered in the mode of comedy. Going to university, as Christopher Marlowe did, was all well and good for honing the arts of rhetorical elaboration and classical allusion, but it could lead to a loss of the common touch. To stay close to a large segment of the potential audience for public theatre, it was necessary to write for clowns as well as kings and to intersperse the flights of poetry with the humour of the tavern, the privy and the brothel: Shakespeare was the first to establish himself early in his career as an equal master of tragedy, comedy and history. He realized that theatre could be the medium to make the national past available to a wider audience than the elite who could afford to read large history books: his signature early works include not only the classical tragedy *Titus Andronicus* but also the sequence of English historical plays on the Wars of the Roses.

He also invented a new role for himself, that of in-house company dramatist. Where his peers and predecessors had to sell their plays to the theatre managers on a poorly-paid piecework basis, Shakespeare took a percentage of the box-office income. The Lord Chamberlain's Men constituted themselves in 1594 as a joint stock company, with the profits being distributed among the core actors who had invested as sharers. Shakespeare acted himself – he appears in the cast lists of some of Ben Jonson's plays as well as the list of actors' names at the beginning of his own collected works – but his principal duty was to write two or three plays a year for the company. By holding shares, he was effectively earning himself a royalty on his work, something no author had ever done before in England. When the Lord Chamberlain's Men collected their fee for performance at court in the Christmas season of 1594, three of them went along to the Treasurer of the Chamber: not just Richard

Burbage the tragedian and Will Kempe the clown, but also Shakespeare the scriptwriter. That was something new.

The next four years were the golden period in Shakespeare's career, though overshadowed by the death of his only son Hamnet, aged eleven, in 1596. In his early thirties and in full command of both his poetic and his theatrical medium, he perfected his art of comedy, while also developing his tragic and historical writing in new ways. In 1598, Francis Meres, a Cambridge University graduate with his finger on the pulse of the London literary world, praised Shakespeare for his excellence across the genres:

> As Plautus and Seneca are accounted the best for comedy and tragedy among the Latins, so Shakespeare among the English is the most excellent in both kinds for the stage; for comedy, witness his *Gentlemen of Verona*, his *Errors*, his *Love Labours Lost*, his *Love Labours Won*, his *Midsummer Night Dream* and his *Merchant of Venice*: for tragedy his *Richard the 2*, *Richard the 3*, *Henry the 4*, *King John*, *Titus Andronicus* and his *Romeo and Juliet*.

For Meres, as for the many writers who praised the 'honey-flowing vein' of *Venus and Adonis* and *Lucrece*, narrative poems written when the theatres were closed due to plague in 1593–94, Shakespeare was marked above all by his linguistic skill, by the gift of turning elegant poetic phrases.

PLAYHOUSES

Elizabethan playhouses were 'thrust' or 'one-room' theatres. To understand Shakespeare's original theatrical life, we have to forget about the indoor theatre of later times, with its proscenium arch and curtain that would be opened at the beginning and closed at the end of each act. In the proscenium arch theatre, stage and auditorium are effectively two separate rooms: the audience looks from one world into another as if through the imaginary 'fourth wall' framed by the proscenium. The picture-frame stage, together with the elaborate scenic effects and backdrops beyond it, created the illusion of a self-contained world – especially once nineteenth-century developments in the control of artificial lighting meant that the auditorium could be darkened and the spectators made to focus on the lighted stage. Shakespeare, by contrast, wrote for a bare platform stage with a standing audience gathered around it in a courtyard in full daylight. The audience were always conscious of themselves and their fellow-spectators, and they shared the same 'room' as the actors. A sense of immediate presence and the creation of rapport with the audience were all-important. The actor could not afford to imagine he was in a closed world, with silent witnesses dutifully observing him from the darkness.

Shakespeare's theatrical career began at the Rose Theatre in Southwark. The stage was wide and shallow, trapezoid in shape, like a lozenge. This design had a great deal of potential for the theatrical equivalent of cinematic split-screen effects, whereby one group of characters would enter at the door at one end of the tiring-house wall at the back of the stage and another group through the door at the other end, thus creating two rival tableaux. Many of the battle-heavy and faction-filled plays that premiered at the Rose have scenes of just this sort.

At the rear of the Rose stage, there were three capacious exits, each over ten feet wide. Unfortunately, the very limited excavation of a fragmentary portion of the original Globe site, also in 1989, revealed nothing about the stage. The first Globe was built in 1599 with similar proportions to those of another theatre, the Fortune, albeit that the former was polygonal and looked circular, whereas the latter was rectangular. The building contract for the Fortune survives and allows us to infer that the stage of the Globe was probably substantially wider than it was deep (perhaps forty-three feet wide and twenty-seven feet deep). It may well have been tapered at the front, like that of the Rose.

The capacity of the Globe was said to have been enormous, perhaps in excess of three thousand. It has been conjectured that about eight hundred people may have stood in the yard, with two thousand or more in the three layers of covered galleries. The other 'public' playhouses were also of large capacity, whereas the indoor

Blackfriars theatre that Shakespeare's company began using in 1608 – the former refectory of a monastery – had overall internal dimensions of a mere forty-six by sixty feet. It would have made for a much more intimate theatrical experience and had a much smaller capacity, probably of about six hundred people. Since they paid at least sixpence a head, the Blackfriars attracted a more select or 'private' audience. The atmosphere would have been closer to that of an indoor performance before the court in the Whitehall Palace or at Richmond. That Shakespeare always wrote for indoor production at court as well as outdoor performance in the public theatre should make us cautious about inferring, as some scholars have, that the opportunity provided by the intimacy of the Blackfriars led to a significant change towards a 'chamber' style in his last plays – which, besides, were performed at both the Globe and the Blackfriars. After the occupation of the Blackfriars a five-act structure seems to have become more important to Shakespeare. That was because of artificial lighting: there were musical interludes between the acts, while the candles were trimmed and replaced. Again, though, something similar must have been necessary for indoor court performances throughout his career.

Front of house there were the 'gatherers' who collected the money from audience members: a penny to stand in the open-air yard, another penny for a place in the covered galleries, sixpence for the prominent 'lord's rooms' to the side of the stage. In the indoor 'private' theatres, gallants from the audience who fancied making themselves part of the spectacle sat on stools on the edge of the stage itself. Scholars debate as to how widespread this practice was in the public theatres such as the Globe. Once the audience were in place and the money counted, the gatherers were available to be extras on stage. That is one reason why battles and crowd scenes often come later rather than early in Shakespeare's plays. There was no formal prohibition upon performance by women, and there certainly were women among the gatherers, so it is not beyond the bounds of possibility that female crowd members were played by females.

The play began at two o'clock in the afternoon and the theatre had to be cleared by five. After the main show, there would be a jig – which consisted not only of dancing, but also of knockabout comedy (it is the origin of the farcical 'afterpiece' in the eighteenth-century theatre). So the time available for a Shakespeare play was about two and a half hours, somewhere between the 'two hours' traffic' mentioned in the prologue to *Romeo and Juliet* and the 'three hours' spectacle' referred to in the preface to the 1647 Folio of Beaumont and Fletcher's plays. The prologue to a play by Thomas Middleton refers to a thousand lines as 'one hour's words', so the likelihood is that about two and a half thousand, or a maximum of three thousand lines made up the performed text. This is indeed the length of most of Shakespeare's comedies, whereas many of his tragedies and histories are much longer, raising the possibility that he wrote full scripts, possibly with eventual publication in mind, in the full knowledge that the stage version would be heavily cut. The short Quarto texts published in his lifetime – they used to be called 'Bad' Quartos – provide fascinating evidence as to the kind of cutting that probably took place. So, for instance, the First Quarto of *Hamlet* neatly merges two occasions when Hamlet is overheard, the 'Fishmonger' and the 'nunnery' scenes.

The social composition of the audience was mixed. The poet Sir John Davies wrote of 'A thousand townsmen, gentlemen and whores, / Porters and servingmen' who would 'together throng' at the public playhouses. Though moralists associated female play-going with adultery and the sex trade, many perfectly respectable citizens' wives were regular attendees. Some, no doubt, resembled the modern groupie: a story attested in two different sources has one citizen's wife making a post-show assignation with Richard Burbage and ending up in bed with Shakespeare – supposedly eliciting from the latter the quip that William the Conqueror was before Richard III. Defenders of theatre liked to say that by witnessing the comeuppance of villains on the stage, audience members would repent of their own wrongdoings, but the reality is that most people went to the theatre then, as they do now, for entertainment more than moral edification. Besides, it would be foolish to suppose that audiences behaved in a homogeneous way: a pamphlet of the 1630s tells of how two men went to see *Pericles* and one of them laughed while the other wept. Bishop John Hall complained that people went to church for the same reasons that they went to the theatre: 'for company, for custom, for recreation ... to feed his eyes or his ears ... or perhaps for sleep'.

Men-about-town and clever young lawyers went to be seen as much as to see. In the modern popular imagination, shaped not least by *Shakespeare in Love* and the opening sequence of Laurence Olivier's *Henry V* film, the penny-paying groundlings stand in the yard hurling abuse or encouragement and hazelnuts or orange peel at the actors, while the sophisticates in the covered galleries appreciate Shakespeare's soaring poetry. The reality was probably the other way round. A 'groundling' was a kind of fish, so the nickname suggests the penny audience standing below the level of the stage and gazing in silent open-mouthed wonder at the spectacle unfolding above them. The more difficult audience members, who kept up a running commentary of clever remarks on the performance and who occasionally got into quarrels with players, were the gallants. Like Hollywood movies in modern times, Elizabethan and Jacobean plays exercised a powerful influence on the fashion and behaviour of the young. John Marston mocks the lawyers who would open their lips, perhaps to court a girl, and out would 'flow / Naught but pure Juliet and Romeo'.

THE ENSEMBLE AT WORK

In the absence of typewriters and photocopying machines, reading aloud would have been the means by which the company got to know a new play. The tradition of the playwright reading his complete script to the assembled company endured for generations. A copy would then have been taken to the Master of the Revels for licensing. The theatre book-holder or prompter would then have copied the parts for distribution to the actors. A partbook consisted of the character's lines, with each speech preceded by the last three or four words of the speech before, the so-called 'cue'. These would have been taken away and studied or 'conned'. During this period of learning the parts, an actor might have had some one-to-one

8. Hypothetical reconstruction of the interior of an Elizabethan playhouse during a performance.

instruction, perhaps from the dramatist, perhaps from a senior actor who had played the same part before, and, in the case of an apprentice, from his master. A high percentage of Desdemona's lines occur in dialogue with Othello, of Lady Macbeth's with Macbeth, Cleopatra's with Antony and Volumnia's with Coriolanus. The roles would almost certainly have been taken by the apprentice of the lead actor, usually Burbage, who delivers the majority of the cues. Given that apprentices lodged with their masters, there would have been ample opportunity for personal instruction, which may be what made it possible for young men to play such demanding parts.

After the parts were learned, there may have been no more than a single rehearsal before the first performance. With six different plays to be put on every week, there was no time for more. Actors, then, would go into a show with a very limited sense of the whole. The notion of a collective rehearsal process that is itself a process of discovery for the actors is wholly modern and would have been incomprehensible to Shakespeare and his original ensemble. Given the number of parts an actor had to hold in his memory, the forgetting of lines was probably more frequent than in the modern theatre. The book-holder was on hand to prompt.

Backstage personnel included the property man, the tire-man who oversaw the costumes, call-boys, attendants and the musicians, who might play at various times from the main stage, the rooms above and within the tiring-house. Scriptwriters sometimes made a nuisance of themselves backstage. There was often tension between the acting companies and the freelance playwrights from whom they purchased scripts: it was a smart move on the part of Shakespeare and the Lord Chamberlain's Men to bring the writing process in-house.

Scenery was limited, though sometimes set-pieces were brought on (a bank of flowers, a bed, the mouth of hell). The trapdoor from below, the gallery stage above and the curtained discovery-space at the back allowed for an array of special effects: the rising of ghosts and apparitions, the descent of gods, dialogue between a character at a window and another at ground level, the revelation of a statue or a pair of lovers playing at chess. Ingenious use could be made of props, as with the ass's head in *A Midsummer Night's Dream*. In a theatre that does not clutter the stage with the material paraphernalia of everyday life, those objects that are deployed may take on powerful symbolic weight, as when Shylock bears his weighing scales in one hand and knife in the other, thus becoming a parody of the figure of Justice who traditionally bears a sword and a balance. Among the more significant items in the property cupboard of Shakespeare's company, there would have been a throne (the 'chair of state'), joint stools, books, bottles, coins, purses, letters (which are brought on stage, read or referred to on about eighty occasions in the complete works), maps, gloves, a set of stocks (in which Kent is put in *King Lear*), rings, rapiers, daggers, broadswords, staves, pistols, masks and vizards, heads and skulls, torches and tapers and lanterns which served to signal night scenes on the daylit stage, a buck's head, an ass's head, animal costumes. Live animals also put in appearances, most notably the dog Crab in *The*

Two Gentlemen of Verona and possibly a young polar bear in *The Winter's Tale*.

The costumes were the most important visual dimension of the play. Playwrights were paid between £2 and £6 per script, whereas Alleyn was not averse to paying £20 for 'a black velvet cloak with sleeves embroidered all with silver and gold'. No matter the period of the play, actors always wore contemporary costume. The excitement for the audience came not from any impression of historical accuracy, but from the richness of the attire and perhaps the transgressive thrill of the knowledge that here were commoners like themselves strutting in the costumes of courtiers in effective defiance of the strict sumptuary laws whereby in real life people had to wear the clothes that befitted their social station.

To an even greater degree than props, costumes could carry symbolic importance. Racial characteristics could be suggested: a breastplate and helmet for a Roman soldier, a turban for a Turk, long robes for exotic characters such as Moors, a gabardine for a Jew. The figure of Time, as in *The Winter's Tale*, would be equipped with hourglass, scythe and wings; Rumour, who speaks the prologue of *2 Henry IV*, wore a costume adorned with a thousand tongues. The wardrobe in the tiring-house of the Globe would have contained much of the same stock as that of rival manager Philip Henslowe at the Rose: green gowns for outlaws and foresters, black for melancholy men such as Jaques and people in mourning such as the Countess in *All's Well that Ends Well* (at the beginning of *Hamlet*, the prince is still in mourning black when everyone else is in festive garb for the wedding of the new king), a gown and hood for a friar (or a feigned friar like the duke in *Measure for Measure*), blue coats and tawny to distinguish the followers of rival factions, a leather apron and ruler for a carpenter (as in the opening scene of *Julius Caesar* – and in *A Midsummer Night's Dream*, where this is the only sign that Peter Quince is a carpenter), a cockle hat with staff and a pair of sandals for a pilgrim or palmer (the disguise assumed by Helen in *All's Well*), bodices and kirtles with farthingales beneath for the boys who are to be dressed as girls. A gender switch such as that of Rosalind or Jessica seems to have taken between fifty and eighty lines of dialogue – Viola does not resume her 'maiden weeds', but remains in her boy's costume to the end of *Twelfth Night* because a change would have slowed down the action at just the moment it was speeding to a climax. Henslowe's inventory also included 'a robe for to go invisible': Oberon, Puck and Ariel must have had something similar.

As the costumes appealed to the eyes, so there was music for the ears. Comedies included many songs. Desdemona's willow song, perhaps a late addition to the text, is a rare and thus exceptionally poignant example from tragedy. Trumpets and tuckets sounded for ceremonial entrances, drums denoted an army on the march. Background music could create atmosphere, as at the beginning of *Twelfth Night*, during the lovers' dialogue near the end of *The Merchant of Venice*, when the statue seemingly comes to life in *The Winter's Tale*, and for the revival of Pericles and of Lear (in the Quarto text, but not the Folio). The haunting sound of the hautboy suggested a realm beyond the human, as when the god Hercules is imagined deserting Mark Antony. Dances symbolized the harmony of the end of a comedy – though in Shakespeare's world of mingled joy and sorrow, someone is usually left out of the circle.

The most important resource was, of course, the actors themselves. They needed many skills: in the words of one contemporary commentator, 'dancing, activity, music, song, elocution, ability of body, memory, skill of weapon, pregnancy of wit'. Their bodies were as significant as their voices. Hamlet tells the player to 'suit the action to the word, the word to the action': moments of strong emotion, known as 'passions', relied on a repertoire of dramatic gestures as well as a modulation of the voice. When Titus Andronicus has had his hand chopped off, he asks 'How can I grace my talk, / Wanting a hand to give it action?' A pen portrait of 'The Character of an Excellent Actor' by the dramatist John Webster is almost certainly based on his impression of Shakespeare's leading man, Richard Burbage: 'By a full and significant action of body, he charms our attention: sit in a full theatre, and you will think you see so many lines drawn from the circumference of so many ears, whiles the actor is the centre . . . .'

Though Burbage was admired above all others, praise was also heaped upon the apprentice players whose alto voices fitted them for the parts of women. A spectator at Oxford in 1610 records how the audience were reduced to tears by the pathos of Desdemona's death. The puritans who fumed about the biblical prohibition upon cross-dressing and the encouragement to sodomy constituted by the sight of an adult male kissing a teenage boy on stage were a small minority. Little is known, however, about the characteristics of the leading apprentices in Shakespeare's company. It may perhaps be inferred that one was a lot taller than the other, since Shakespeare often wrote for a pair of female friends, one tall and fair, the other short and dark (Helena and Hermia, Rosalind and Celia, Beatrice and Hero).

We know little about Shakespeare's own acting roles – an early allusion indicates that he often took royal parts, and a venerable tradition gives him old Adam in *As You Like It* and the ghost of old King Hamlet. Save for Burbage's lead roles and the generic part of the clown, all such castings are mere speculation. We do not even know for sure whether the original Falstaff was Will Kempe or another actor who specialized in comic roles, Thomas Pope.

Kempe left the company in early 1599. Tradition has it that he fell out with Shakespeare over the matter of excessive improvisation. He was replaced by Robert Armin, who was less of a clown and more of a cerebral wit: this explains the difference between such parts as Lancelet Gobbo and Dogberry, which were written for Kempe, and the more verbally sophisticated Feste and Lear's Fool, which were written for Armin.

One thing that is clear from surviving 'plots' or story-boards of plays from the period is that a degree of doubling was necessary. *2 Henry VI* has over sixty speaking parts, but more than half of the characters only appear in a single scene and most scenes have only six to eight speakers. At a stretch, the play could be performed by thirteen actors. When Thomas Platter saw *Julius Caesar* at the Globe in 1599, he noted that there were about fifteen. Why doesn't Paris go to the Capulet ball in *Romeo and Juliet*? Perhaps because he was doubled with Mercutio, who does. In *The Winter's Tale*, Mamillius might have come back as Perdita and Antigonus been doubled by Camillo, making the partnership with Paulina at the end a very neat touch. Titania and Oberon are often played by the same pair as Hippolyta and Theseus, suggesting a symbolic matching of the rulers of the worlds of night and day, but it is questionable whether there would have been time for the necessary costume changes. As so often, one is left in a realm of tantalizing speculation.

THE KING'S MAN

The new king, James I, who had held the Scottish throne as James VI since he had been an infant, immediately took the Lord Chamberlain's Men under his direct patronage. Henceforth they would be the King's Men, and for the rest of Shakespeare's career they were favoured with far more court performances than any of their rivals. There even seem to have been rumours early in the reign that Shakespeare and Burbage were being considered for knighthoods, an unprecedented honour for mere actors – and one that in the event was not accorded to a member of the profession for nearly three hundred years, when the title was bestowed upon Henry Irving, the leading Shakespearean actor of Queen Victoria's reign.

Shakespeare's productivity rate slowed in the Jacobean years, not because of age or some personal trauma, but because there were frequent outbreaks of plague, causing the theatres to be closed for long periods. The King's Men were forced to spend many months on the road. Between November 1603 and 1608, they were to be found at various towns in the south and Midlands, though Shakespeare probably did not tour with them by this time. He had bought a large house back home in Stratford and was accumulating other property. He may indeed have stopped acting soon after the new king took the throne. With the London theatres closed so much of the time and a large repertoire on the stocks, Shakespeare seems to have focused his energies on writing a few long and complex tragedies that could have been played on demand at court: *Othello*, *King Lear*, *Antony and Cleopatra*, *Coriolanus* and *Cymbeline* are among his longest and poetically grandest plays. *Macbeth* only survives in a shorter text, which shows signs of adaptation after Shakespeare's death. The bitterly satirical *Timon of Athens*, apparently a collaboration with Thomas Middleton that may have failed on the stage, also belongs to this period. In comedy, too, he wrote longer and morally darker works than in the Elizabethan period, pushing at the very bounds of the form in *Measure for Measure* and *All's Well that Ends Well*.

From 1608 onwards, when the King's Men began occupying the indoor Blackfriars playhouse (as a winter house, meaning that they only used the outdoor Globe in summer?), Shakespeare turned to a more romantic style. His company had a great success with a revived and altered version of an old pastoral play called *Mucedorus*. It even featured a bear. The younger dramatist John Fletcher, meanwhile, sometimes working in collaboration with Francis Beaumont, was pioneering a new style of tragicomedy, a mix of romance and royalism laced with intrigue and pastoral excursions. Shakespeare experimented with this idiom in *Cymbeline* and it was presumably with his blessing that Fletcher eventually took over as the King's Men's company dramatist. The two writers apparently collaborated on three plays in the years 1612–14: a lost romance called *Cardenio* (based on the love-madness of a character in Cervantes' *Don Quixote*), *Henry VIII* (originally staged with the title 'All is True'), and *The Two Noble Kinsmen*, a dramatization of Chaucer's 'Knight's Tale' These were written after Shakespeare's two final solo-authored plays, *The Winter's Tale*, a self-consciously old-fashioned work dramatizing the pastoral romance of his old enemy Robert Greene, and *The Tempest*, which at one and the same time drew together multiple theatrical traditions, diverse reading and contemporary interest in the fate of a ship that had been wrecked on the way to the New World.

The collaborations with Fletcher suggest that Shakespeare's career ended with a slow fade rather than the sudden retirement supposed by the nineteenth-century Romantic critics who read Prospero's epilogue to *The Tempest* as Shakespeare's personal farewell to his art. In the last few years of his life Shakespeare certainly spent more of his time in Stratford-upon-Avon, where he became further involved in property dealing and litigation. But his London life also continued. In 1613 he made his first major London property purchase: a freehold house in the Blackfriars district, close to his company's indoor theatre. *The Two Noble Kinsmen* may have been written as late as 1614, and Shakespeare was in London on business a little over a year before he died of an unknown cause at home in Stratford-upon-Avon in 1616, probably on his fifty-second birthday.

About half the sum of his works were published in his lifetime, in texts of variable quality. A few years after his death, his fellow-actors began putting together an authorized edition of his complete *Comedies, Histories and Tragedies*. It appeared in 1623, in large 'Folio' format. This collection of thirty-six plays gave Shakespeare his immortality. In the words of his fellow-dramatist Ben Jonson, who contributed two poems of praise at the start of the Folio, the body of his work made him 'a monument without a tomb':

> And art alive still while thy book doth live
> And we have wits to read and praise to give ...
> He was not of an age, but for all time!

SHAKESPEARE'S WORKS: A CHRONOLOGY

1589–91	*? Arden of Faversham* (possible part authorship)
1589–92	*The Taming of the Shrew*
1589–92	*? Edward the Third* (possible part authorship)
1591	*The Second Part of Henry the Sixth*, originally called *The First Part of the Contention betwixt the Two Famous Houses of York and Lancaster* (element of co-authorship possible)
1591	*The Third Part of Henry the Sixth*, originally called *The True Tragedy of Richard Duke of York* (element of co-authorship probable)
1591–92	*The Two Gentlemen of Verona*
1591–92; perhaps revised 1594	*The Lamentable Tragedy of Titus Andronicus* (probably co-written with, or revising an earlier version by, George Peele)
1592	*The First Part of Henry the Sixth*, probably with Thomas Nashe and others
1592/94	*King Richard the Third*
1593	*Venus and Adonis* (poem)
1593–94	*The Rape of Lucrece* (poem)
1593–1608	*Sonnets* (154 poems, published 1609 with *A Lover's Complaint*, a poem of disputed authorship)
1592–94/ 1600–03	*Sir Thomas More* (a single scene for a play originally by Anthony Munday, with other revisions by Henry Chettle, Thomas Dekker and Thomas Heywood)
1594	*The Comedy of Errors*
1595	*Love's Labour's Lost*

1595–97	*Love's Labour's Won* (a lost play, unless the original title for another comedy)
1595–96	*A Midsummer Night's Dream*
1595–96	*The Tragedy of Romeo and Juliet*
1595–96	*King Richard the Second*
1595–97	*The Life and Death of King John* (possibly earlier)
1596–97	*The Merchant of Venice*
1596–97	*The First Part of Henry the Fourth*
1597–98	*The Second Part of Henry the Fourth*
1598	*Much Ado about Nothing*
1598–99	*The Passionate Pilgrim* (20 poems, some not by Shakespeare)
1599	*The Life of Henry the Fifth*
1599	'To the Queen' (epilogue for a court performance)
1599	*As You Like It*
1599	*The Tragedy of Julius Caesar*
1600–01	*The Tragedy of Hamlet, Prince of Denmark* (perhaps revising an earlier version)
1600–01	*The Merry Wives of Windsor* (perhaps revising version of 1597–99)
1601	'Let the Bird of Loudest Lay' (poem, known since 1807 as 'The Phoenix and Turtle' (turtle-dove))
1601	*Twelfth Night, or What You Will*
1601–02	*The Tragedy of Troilus and Cressida*
1604	*The Tragedy of Othello, the Moor of Venice*
1604	*Measure for Measure*
1605	*All's Well that Ends Well*
1605	*The Life of Timon of Athens*, with Thomas Middleton
1605–06	*The Tragedy of King Lear*
1605–08	? contribution to *The Four Plays in One* (lost, except for *A Yorkshire Tragedy*, mostly by Thomas Middleton)
1606	*The Tragedy of Macbeth* (surviving text has additional scenes by Thomas Middleton)
1606–07	*The Tragedy of Antony and Cleopatra*
1608	*The Tragedy of Coriolanus*

1608	*Pericles, Prince of Tyre*, with George Wilkins
1610	*The Tragedy of Cymbeline*
1611	*The Winter's Tale*
1611	*The Tempest*
1612–13	*Cardenio*, with John Fletcher (survives only in later adaptation called *Double Falsehood* by Lewis Theobald)
1613	*Henry VIII (All is True)*, with John Fletcher
1613–14	*The Two Noble Kinsmen*, with John Fletcher

FURTHER READING
AND VIEWING

CRITICAL APPROACHES

Barber, C. L., *Shakespeare's Festive Comedy: A Study of Dramatic Form and its Relation to Social Custom* (1959). Half a century after publication, still the best book on Shakespearean comedy.

Calderwood, James L., *A Midsummer Night's Dream* (1992). Good on 'meta-drama', theatrical self-awareness.

Frye, Northrop, *A Natural Perspective: The Development of Shakespearean Comedy and Romance* (1967). Luminous study of Shakespearean comedy that develops 'The Argument of Comedy' (discussed in our introduction, pp. 5–8).

Kehler, Dorothea, ed., *A Midsummer Night's Dream: Critical Essays* (2001). Wide selection of approaches.

Kermode, Frank, 'The Mature Comedies', in *Early Shakespeare*, ed. John Russell Brown and Bernard Harris (1961), pp. 214–20. Characteristically sensitive reading by a great critic.

Kott, Jan, 'Titania and the Ass's Head' in his *Shakespeare Our Contemporary* (1964). Highly influential 'dark' and sexual reading.

Laroque, François, *Shakespeare's Festive World: Elizabethan Seasonal Entertainment and the Professional Stage* (1991). Useful extension of Barber's work.

Levine, Laura, 'Rape, Repetition, and the Politics of Closure in *A Midsummer Night's Dream*', in *Feminist Readings of Early Modern Culture: Emerging Subjects,* ed. Valerie Traub, M. Lindsay Kaplan and Dympna Callaghan (1996), pp. 210–28. An example of a feminist approach.

Montrose, Louis Adrian, *The Purpose of Playing: Shakespeare and the Cultural Politics of the Elizabethan Theatre* (1996), pp. 109–205. Influential 'new historicist' reading.

Patterson, Annabel, 'Bottom's Up: Festive Theory', in *Shakespeare and the Popular Voice* (1989), pp. 52–70. Politically engaged.

Young, David P., *Something of Great Constancy: The Art of 'A Midsummer Night's Dream'* (1966). Thoughtful and detailed.

THE PLAY IN PERFORMANCE

Brooke, Michael, *'A Midsummer Night's Dream'* on Screen, www.screenonline.org.uk/tv/id/564758/index.html. Pithy overview. Registered schools, colleges, universities and libraries have access to video clips, including the complete twelve minutes of the silent 1908 version.

Griffiths, Trevor R., ed., *A Midsummer Night's Dream*, Shakespeare in Production (1996). Much helpful detail.

Halio, Jay L., *A Midsummer Night's Dream*, Shakespeare in Performance (1994). Good survey.

Jacobs, Sally, 'Designing the Dream', in *Peter Brook's Production of William Shakespeare's 'A Midsummer Night's Dream' for the Royal Shakespeare Company: The Complete and Authorised Acting Edition*, ed. Glen Loney (1974). Insider's voice.

McArdle, Aidan, 'Puck (and Philostrate)', in *Players of Shakespeare 5*, ed. Robert Smallwood (2003). Perceptive actor's view.

RSC 'Exploring Shakespeare: *A Midsummer Night's Dream*', www.rsc.org.uk/explore/plays/dream.htm. Particular focus on the multilingual Dash Arts production directed by Tim Supple.

Selbourne, David, *The Making of A Midsummer Night's Dream: An Eye-Witness Account of Peter Brook's Production from First Rehearsal to First Night* (1982). Invaluable record of the seminal production.

Styan, J. L., *The Shakespeare Revolution: Criticism and Performance in the Twentieth Century* (1976). Good on changing production styles and relationship between criticism and theatre.

Warren, Roger, *A Midsummer Night's Dream*, Text and Performance (1983). Useful.

Williams, Gary Jay, *Our Moonlight Revels: A Midsummer Night's Dream in the Theatre* (1997). Overview of stage history.

For a more detailed Shakespeare bibliography and selections from a wide range of critical accounts of the play, with linking commentary, visit the edition website, www.rscshakespeare.co.uk.

AVAILABLE ON DVD

A Midsummer Night's Dream, directed by Charles Kent and J. Stuart Blackton (1909, on DVD *Silent Shakespeare*, 2004). Short silent version, nicely exploiting the technological 'magic' of the new medium of film.

A Midsummer Night's Dream, directed by William Dieterle and Max Reinhardt (1935, DVD 2007). One of the all-time classic Shakespeare films, with James Cagney as Bottom and Mickey Rooney as Puck.

A Midsummer Night's Dream, directed by Peter Hall (1968, DVD 2005). Television broadcast of an exemplary RSC production, with Ian Richardson (Oberon), Judi Dench (Titania), David Warner (Lysander), Diana Rigg (Helena), Helen Mirren (Hermia) and Ian Holm (Puck).

A Midsummer Night's Dream, directed by Elijah Moshinsky (1981, DVD 2004). Despite Helen Mirren's presence as Titania, a weak made-for-television production in the BBC complete Shakespeare series.

A Midsummer Night's Dream, directed by Adrian Noble (1996, DVD 2001). Film adaptation of RSC stage production.

A Midsummer Night's Dream, directed by Michael Hoffman (1999, DVD 2002). Patchy, despite (or because of) strong Hollywood cast, including Kevin Kline as Bottom and Michelle Pfeiffer as Titania.

The Children's Midsummer Night's Dream, directed by Christine Edzard (2001, DVD 2006). Is what it says it is: acted (with varying degrees of success) by children.

REFERENCES

1 E. K. Chambers, *The Elizabethan Stage* (4 vols, 1924), Vol. 3, p. 279.
2 William A. Ringler, Jr, 'The Number of Actors in Shakespeare's Early Plays', in *The Seventeenth-Century Stage*, ed. G. E. Bentley (1968), p. 134.
3 *Bottom the Weaver* (1661, facsimile repr. 1970), sig. a2v.
4 *The Diary of Samuel Pepys*, ed. Robert Latham and William Matthews (11 vols, 1970–82), Vol. 3, p. 208 (29 September 1662).
5 William Hazlitt, *Characters of Shakespear's Plays* (1817), pp. 126–34.
6 Playbills, Theatre Museum, London.
7 Jay Halio, *A Midsummer Night's Dream*, Shakespeare in Performance (1994), pp. 30–1.
8 Ellen Terry, *Memoirs* (1933), p. 149.
9 *The Times*, review of *A Midsummer Night's Dream*, 11 January 1900.
10 Harley Granville-Barker, *Prefaces to Shakespeare* (2 vols, 1946–47), Vol. 2, p. 346.
11 François Laroque, *Shakespeare's Festive World* (1991), p. 122.
12 Peter Brook, interview with Peter Ansorge, *Plays and Players*, October 1970.
13 Brook, interview with Ansorge.
14 Halio, *A Midsummer Night's Dream*, p. 31.
15 Trevor R. Griffiths, *A Midsummer Night's Dream*, Shakespeare in Production (1996), p. 72.
16 Halio, *A Midsummer Night's Dream*, p. 59.
17 Edgar Allan Poe, *A Dream Within a Dream* (1827).
18 J. C. Trewin, *Illustrated London News*, 12 September 1970.
19 Sally Jacobs, 'Designing the Dream', in *Peter Brook's Production of William Shakespeare's 'A Midsummer Night's Dream' for the Royal Shakespeare Company: The Complete and Authorised Acting Edition* (1974).
20 J. L. Styan, *The Shakespeare Revolution: Criticism and Performance in the Twentieth Century* (1977), p. 167.
21 Peter Brook, interview with Ronald Hayman, *The Times*, 29 August 1970.
22 Irving Wardle, *The Times*, 28 August 1970.
23 Styan, *The Shakespeare Revolution*, p. 169.
24 Adrian Noble, *A Midsummer Night's Dream*, RSC Education Pack (1994).
25 Charles Spencer, *Daily Telegraph*, 5 August 1994.
26 Anthony Ward, *A Midsummer Night's Dream*, RSC Education Pack (1994).
27 Michael Billington, *Guardian*, 5 August 1994.
28 Benedict Nightingale, *The Times*, 5 August 1994.
29 Chris Parry, *A Midsummer Night's Dream*, RSC Education Pack (1994).
30 D. H. Lawrence, *Autumn Sunshine* (1916).
31 Gavin Millar, *Listener*, 3 September 1970.
32 Michael Billington, *Guardian*, 21 February 2002.
33 Patrick Carnegy, *Spectator*, 2 March 2002.
34 Benedict Nightingale, *The Times*, 21 February 2002.

35 Michael Billington, *Guardian*, 21 February 2002.
36 Susannah Clapp, *Observer*, 24 February 2002.
37 Halio, *A Midsummer Night's Dream*, p. 66.
38 Gary Jay Williams, *Theatre*, Summer–Fall, 1982.
39 Benedict Nightingale, *New Statesman*, 24 July 1981.
40 Charles Spencer, *Daily Telegraph*, 16 April 2005.
41 Nicholas de Jongh, *Evening Standard*, 18 April 2005.
42 Patrick Carnegy, *Spectator*, 23 April 2005.
43 Stanley Wells, note for *A Midsummer Night's Dream*, RSC programme, 1970.
44 Brook, interview with Ansorge.
45 Eric Shorter, *Daily Telegraph*, 9 July 1986.
46 Michael Coveney, *Financial Times*, 9 July 1986.
47 Lyn Gardner, *City Limits*, 17 July 1986.
48 Jim Hiley, *Listener*, 17 July 1986.
49 Halio, *A Midsummer Night's Dream*, p. 97.
50 Benedict Nightingale, *The Times*, 29 March 1999.
51 Aidan McArdle, 'Puck (and Philostrate)', in *Players of Shakespeare* 5, ed. Robert Smallwood (2003), p. 49.
52 McArdle, 'Puck (and Philostrate)', p. 51.
53 McArdle, 'Puck (and Philostrate)', p. 52.
54 Stubbes, quoted in C. L. Barber's brilliant account of *Shakespeare's Festive Comedy* (1959), pp. 21–2.
55 James Sully, programme note in *A Midsummer Night's Dream*, RSC Programme, 1984.
56 Helen Dawson, *Observer*, 30 August 1970.
57 Mary Z. Maher, '*A Midsummer Night's Dream*: Nightmare or Gentle Snooze?', in *A Midsummer Night's Dream: Critical Essays*, ed. Dorothea Kehler (1998), p. 364.
58 Michael Boyd, interview with Rex Gibson, *Times Education Supplement*, 22 March 1999.
59 Benedict Nightingale, *The Times*, 29 March 1999.

ACKNOWLEDGEMENTS AND PICTURE CREDITS

Preparation of 'A Midsummer Night's Dream in Performance' was assisted by a generous grant from the CAPITAL Centre (Creativity and Performance in Teaching and Learning) of the University of Warwick for research in the RSC archive at the Shakespeare Birthplace Trust. The Arts and Humanities Research Council (AHRC) funded a term's research leave that enabled Jonathan Bate to work on 'The Director's Cut'.

Picture research by Helen Robson and Jan Sewell. Grateful acknowledgement is made to the Shakespeare Birthplace Trust for assistance with picture research (special thanks to Helen Hargest) and reproduction fees.

Images of RSC productions are supplied by the Shakespeare Centre Library and Archive, Stratford-upon-Avon. This Library, maintained by the Shakespeare Birthplace Trust, holds the most important collection of Shakespeare material in the UK, including the Royal Shakespeare Company's official archives. It is open to the public free of charge.

For more information see www.shakespeare.org.uk.

1. Princess Theatre (1856) Reproduced by permission of the Shakespeare Birthplace Trust
2. Mary Ure and Robert Hardy (1959) Angus McBean © Royal Shakespeare Company
3. Directed by Peter Brook (1970) Joe Cocks Studio Collection © Shakespeare Birthplace Trust
4. Directed by Tim Supple (2006) Suzanne Worthington © Royal Shakespeare Company

FROM THE ROYAL SHAKESPEARE COMPANY
AND MACMILLAN

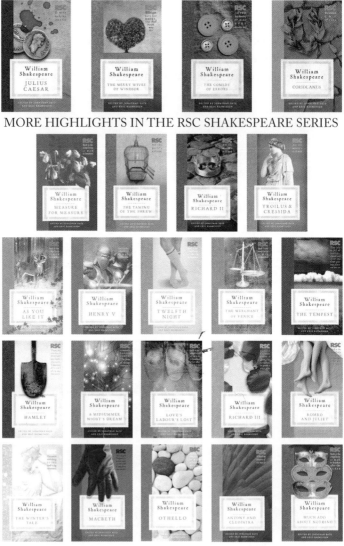

MORE HIGHLIGHTS IN THE RSC SHAKESPEARE SERIES